The Press
and the Decline
of
Democracy

The Press and the Decline of Democracy

THE DEMOCRATIC SOCIALIST RESPONSE IN PUBLIC POLICY

Robert G. Picard

CONTRIBUTIONS TO THE STUDY OF MASS
MEDIA AND COMMUNICATIONS, NUMBER 4

GREENWOOD PRESS
WESTPORT, CONNECTICUT · LONDON, ENGLAND

Library of Congress Cataloging in Publication Data

Picard, Robert G.
  The press and the decline of democracy.

  (Contributions to the study of mass media and
communications, ISSN 0732-4456 ; no. 4)
  Bibliography: p.
Includes index.
  1. Democracy.   2. Political participation.
3. Journalism—Political aspects.   I. Title.   II. Series.
JC423.P45   1985   321.8   85-5585
ISBN 0-313-24915-6 (lib. bdg. : alk. paper)

Library of Congress Catalog Card Number: 85-5585
ISBN: 0-313-24915-6
ISSN: 0732-4456

First published in 1985

Greenwood Press
A division of Congressional Information Service, Inc.
88 Post Road West
Westport, Connecticut 06881

Printed in the United States of America

10 9 8 7 6 5 4 3 2 1

To Elizabeth

Contents

Figures and Tables

FIGURES

TABLES

Acknowledgments

This book was completed with the help, encouragement, and nagging of dozens of friends, colleagues, and advisors. Special thanks go to Paul Fisher and John Merrill for their encouragement. Paul asked probing and critical questions during the development of the ideas for this book and disagreed with me much of the way. John, who often disagrees with me as well, helped hone my views and regularly critiqued my ideas and suggested readings.

I also want to acknowledge the assistance rendered by J. Herbert Altschull, Elizabeth L. Carpelan, and Patrick Parsons, who read the manuscript and offered criticism and suggestions that led to publication.

As the ideas for this book were developed and presented at various conferences and meetings, I received critiques and new directions for research and inquiry from a variety of colleagues, including Hanno Hardt, Clifford Christians, John Soloski, Beverly James, Peter Leo, Murilo Ramos, and Ed McLuskie. I thank them all.

The Press
and the Decline
of
Democracy

1

Democracy and the Role of the Press

It is the average man, the man who doesn't have large corporate interest to protect, that is the strength of a democracy. His reasoning ability and sense of justice enacted into decisions and policies constitute the type of government envisioned by those who wrote America's Declaration of Independence. There has never been a better idea for governing a nation. Our major mistakes have not been the result of democracy, *but of the erosion of democracy made possible by mass media's manipulation of public opinion.*

—Robert Cirino[1]

The ability of the major social institutions to carry out their functions that support democratic rule has been increasingly questioned in the last half of the twentieth century, and the institutions' traditional roles have changed rapidly. Electoral reforms, interest groups, increased interest in public opinion analysis, and press reform movements have all arisen as responses to the growing perception that institutions of democratic government are working less precisely than desired and that the will of the people is not being carried out. As a result of these problems, renewed consideration of the roles of social institutions has begun and new models of democratic governance have appeared.

The role of the press in democracies has come under special scrutiny because of the press's unique functions in the democratic process, functions that grew in importance with the rise of mass society. In the past century, the press has rejected much of its role as a facilitator of political expression or has been forced to give it up because of the rise of capitalistic competition in the newspaper industry. This is not a surprising occurrence, since capitalism and democracy are inherently contradictory concepts. Capitalism sets up structural barriers to the achievement of true democracy and true equality among citizens.

The ideal democracy is based on the absence of inequality of opportunity, whether political, economic, or social. Capitalism, however, is rooted in the creation and promotion of inequality in economic relations. This economic inequality structurally makes it possible for those with wealth to use their economic resources to achieve and maintain political and social inequality by controlling the mechanisms of power. The concentration of political power in the hands of those with wealth is inevitable under capitalism and alien to the concept of full democracy, which requires that privilege not be invested in any particular subgroup of the citizenry.

The ways in which capitalistic activities can harm the interests of democracy can be seen clearly in the press. Until recently, throughout the Western world government policies supporting economic competition in the press have effectively limited public discourse, freedom of expression, and media plurality. These policies have thus contributed to the diminution of the limited democracy in the West today and reduced possibilities for extending participation in society.

Government policies toward the press have, for the most part, favored growth of large, commercial press entities. The few anti-cartel measures that have been enacted have been weak. Tax policies have generally promoted concentration of ownership and the establishment of local monopolies. The lack of stringent antitrust provisions has allowed large newspapers throughout the West to pursue monopolistic marketing strategies in advertising and circulation that have disadvantaged smaller newspapers and forced many out of business.

All of these developments make it more difficult for diverse opinions to be heard and permit elite groups and individuals to have more say on public policies than other, less privileged, members of society. Similar developments in other industries and in public life as a whole have contributed to the rise of democratic socialism in the last half of the twentieth century as a means of combatting the declining amount of participation permitted individuals in all spheres of decision making.

In the ideal democracy, of course, individuals participate equally in the decision-making processes and no one is any more capable of achieving his or her desires through official action than is any other member of the society. The ideal has obviously never been achieved in any society, and the degree to which the ideal is approximated varies over time in any society.

This study accepts the premise that democracy has declined in the Western democratic world in recent decades because public participation in originating policy proposals and deciding public policy has been eroded. This erosion has occurred because of the growth of bureaucracy and technocracy in decision-making apparatuses and because of increasing elite control and manipulation of the vehicles of public opinion and political expression.

The problem of dealing with the normative concept of democracy and the existence of a form that does not achieve the ideal has perplexed political theorists who have attempted to deal with the modes of public conduct in the real world and the purported philosophical bases for this conduct. Filippo Burzio helped pave the way for this new type of political study by arguing:

In a democratic whole we must make a distinction between three diverse elements: 1) a *reality*, that is, rapid circulation of elites; 2) a *desire*, that is equality . . . 3) an *illusion*, that is, direct government of the masses.[2]

In order to more fully comprehend the damaging effects of economic developments in the press, it is important to consider the origins, development, maturation, and endangerment of democracy.

Modern democratic rule emerged in the eighteenth and nineteenth centuries with the breaking of the private franchise on political rights held by the royalty and nobility of Western nations. Rule by the people was not implemented according to a coordinated, universal, Western plan during this great political revolution, but developed slowly, in accordance with the cultural and philosophical conditions present in each nation. Nevertheless, general patterns of development leading to democratic rule existed in the West.[3]

Although the approaches to democratic rule varied from nation to nation, the concerns expressed by citizens remained the same: to set the citizen above the state and to provide maximum liberty for individuals while treating all citizens equally. In reversing the existing political order and making the state the servant of the poeple, it was recognized that the state should be kept from encroaching on the liberties of citizens. A primary liberty that needs protection for democratic rule to succeed is liberty of expression—the right of individuals to speak and write freely, with a minimum of legal controls, on topics and issues with which they are concerned.

During the democratic revolutions that broke monarchical rule and continued the disintegration of the feudal order in the eighteenth and nineteenth centuries, the framers of most documents of democratic rule employed passages that forbade the state from encroaching on certain enumerated and unenumerated liberties. Generally these liberties included those believed to be the basis of democratic rule: the liberty to assemble, the liberty to speak, and the liberty to publish. These freedoms were afforded enumerated protections because they were recognized as links between the citizen and authorities, links that were necessary if citizens were to make learned decisions and conduct a democratic society.

As theories of democratic rule were postulated and debated, the necessity of dealing with the tension created by adherence to the sometimes contradictory concepts of liberty and equality became clear, and theorists began seeking means of accommodating the two concepts. In seeking to provide liberty, the creators of modern democracies sought to minimize external restraints on citizens while providing them with equal opportunity to participate in democratic society.[4]

In seeking to accommodate these two principles of democratic rule, most modern democratic states were constituted with

forms of representative democracy, wherein the people dele-
gated political authority to public servants to carry out the tasks
of government. In these forms of government, representatives
selected by the electorate were empowered to make decisions,
but generally were not bound to vote the will of the people.
The devices intended to link citizens to their representatives,
and thus make the representatives responsive to the will of the
people, were elections, political organizations, and public opinion generated and conveyed through the press.[5]

Representative democracy was selected as the major form of
government because many of the architects of the new democratic states, chiefly representatives of the nobility and the rising economic aristocracy, feared the potential consequences of
direct democracy. Direct democracy would employ widespread
citizen participation and not create the separation between the
rulers and the ruled found in representative systems. It would
also reduce the influence of members of the aristocracy and nobility by giving greater voice to the mass of citizens.[6]

Although significant support existed for direct democracy in
the rule of townships and in small governments in the eighteenth and nineteenth centuries, the concept was not adopted
for larger governments because of the problems it appeared to
present in reconciling majority rule with minority rights. As a
result, many settled for what Robert A. Dahl terms "Madison-
ian Democracy," a compromise between the power of minorities and the power of majorities.[7] The protection of minority
rights was a particular concern of the fathers of democratic
governments, in part because of their wishes to protect the
privileges of property and wealth that would be enjoyed by the
minority in the new "democracies."

In the practice of representative government, a system of
limited majoritarian rule was implemented as an alternative to
direct democracy. During the founding of modern democracies, there was a fear that the mass of citizens would restrict
minority property and political rights. This, along with lack of
the widespread communication that was necessary for direct rule,
thwarted hopes for direct participation in government. Representative majoritarian rule thus seemed a pragmatic method of
dealing with the lack of consensus in society, but the operation

of such rule was generally limited to clearly political issues and not extended to social and economic issues.

Although representative government seemed a practical method of dealing with the problems caused by the inability to provide citizens with the information necessary for making decisions and for fully voicing their views, it contravened the concept of equality because, while it protected some minority rights, it did not provide equal representation for those not holding the prevailing viewpoints.[8] To address this difficulty, representative systems were generally organized so that they provided some avenues for other views to be considered.

As changes and improvements in communication in the nineteenth century began to create mass society in ways that could not have been imagined a century before, new techniques and media for persuasion and for conveying information and ideas to and from the mass of citizens became available. The resulting creation of mass societies helped renew calls, especially from the scholars of the Chicago School, for more direct participation in decision making; the increased communication made it possible for citizens to receive information necessary to make decisions and to convey their wishes more directly to public servants.

By the middle of the twentieth century, arguments for more participation grew even stronger because of the changing relationship between the state and economics. As states began participating heavily in and directing economic planning and policymaking, blending socialistic policies into capitalism as a means of ameliorating the harmful effects of industrial capitalism, citizens began to seek more participation in such activities. They argued that since state action was involved, the mass of citizens and not just the economic elites should participate in making the decisions. As a result, economic planning and policymaking were introduced more directly into the democratically ruled political arena in much of the West.[9]

Despite these past improvements in democratic governance, no direct democracies are found in the world today. Some limited means for promoting participation in decision making in areas of social and economic planning have been instituted in most Western nations and some progressive socialist states, but participation has not been extended to all realms of political, social, and economic life to the point that direct democracy, or even a fully representative democracy, has been achieved.

Political strategies that advocated state regulation or ownership of the most important means of production, distribution, and exchange were increasingly adopted in the West. After the Second World War, even supporters of liberal democracy advocated and supported increased political direction of economic and social life in general.

In practice, the political and economic systems of the West are now inseparable, and political power is inextricably tied to economic power. Concurrently with this development, government and political apparatuses have grown and have come under the control of bureaucratic and elite groups. This control has been recently documented and explored by such scholars as Thomas Dye, John Pickering, and G. William Domhoff.[10] As a result of such studies and increased awareness of policy decisions made by elites, there is a widespread public perception that governments place the interests of business and members of the ruling elites above the interests of the average citizen.

It is now clear that democratic theory and practice have been significantly altered during the past three centuries. While early theorists were most concerned with the values and norms of democracies, modern theorists are more concerned with describing and explaining existing democratic practices and seeking means of achieving democratic goals. These theorists seek means of transforming current practices into ones that support wide citizen participation, i.e., into practices that more closely approximate the democratic ideal.

Democracy is a widely misunderstood and misused word today. It carries little shared meaning because it is often employed to denote not only an ideological concept but a process as well. Democracy can best be described as the *ideal* that all members of a society should collectively decide how society is operated and regulated. The term *democratic rule*, however, is best used to describe the reality, the *process* of citizen participation in decision making. This process can be instituted in varying degrees. The amount of participation by citizens, the scope of activities in which participation is permitted, and the constraints on how participation is exercised determine the extent to which there is democratic rule. If there are limits to the areas in which democratic participation is permitted and the ways it may operate, and these limits are put in place and maintained by factors other than the general will of the greater mass of people, then the ideal of democracy has not been achieved. However, a *form* of democratic rule may exist.[11]

True democracy can exist only when the widest possible participation is afforded in all institutions that affect society at large. This presupposes that no one or no external factors shall determine that an individual do or be something, or not be able to do or be something, unless it is communally agreed to be in the greater interest of society and regulations to that effect apply equally to all citizens.

The concept of participation is basic to the concepts of democracy and democratic rule. It denotes the sharing of decision making among all those involved in or affected by the area in which decisions are made. Most of the democratic revolutions of the eighteenth and nineteenth centuries focused on political democracy, the distribution of political power within the citizenry. But participation and democracy can be taken much further. In social democracy, for instance, the democratization of society itself is sought, and attempts are made to level status differences in society. In the West, the most significant attempts to level social differences have been made in Scandinavia. Democracy can also be sought in the economic area, where it manifests itself in attempts to equalize wealth and economic opportunity. Minimal attempts to achieve a degree of economic equality or opportunity are found in Sweden and a few other Western states, and they have usually involved tax policies as a means of redistributing wealth. Because those efforts have been limited, no significant progress toward achieving economic democracy has been made. Related to economic democracy is the concept of industrial democracy, which manifests itself in worker participation in the management of industrial facilities. Policies promoting such participation are called "co-determination" in Germany and Austria and "self-management" in Yugoslavia, which has undertaken significant experimentation with the concept. Industrial democracy has also been manifest in joint planning of production by management and trade unions throughout most of Europe since the Second World War.[12]

Only when individuals participate significantly in decision making in all areas of political, social, and economic life can true democracy be realized. Thus, it must be recognized that no nation today has achieved democracy in its grandest sense, although some are making efforts to increase participation—efforts especially apropos because of the increasingly technocratic and bureaucratic nature of the political machinery.

The instruments through which true democracy is made possible are those rights and privileges that protect individual liberty and individuals' ability to seek self-realization. The protection of minorities and minority rights is not alien to this broad concept of democracy—for even in true democracy there would be division into majority and minority groups—but neither is the protection of the majority and majority rights from abuse of power by that minority with economic means and elite status.

Under the banner of the "social contract," the basis upon which civil society is created, political philosophers of the sixteenth and seventeenth centuries asserted the justification for constitutional liberalism, the guiding principle of modern democratic governance. Drawing from early Greek manifestations of the concept, Hobbes and Locke argued that the social contract defines the rights and duties within states by placing boundaries on the behavior of citizens and rulers. Rousseau asserted that in entering the contract, individuals surrender some of their rights to the state and commit themselves to abiding by the decisions of the government in those areas.

The social contract has its greatest meaning to those involved in establishing new political orders and the basic rules of a new society. Those who enter the society later, through birth, immigration, or cession, inherit the agreement and are expected to adhere to the contract. The boundaries of the contract are stipulated in law, social norms, and the prevailing philosophy of the society.

In the social contract of a truly democratic society, the individual gives up only such rights as are important to the development and maintenance of the society. Under this view, no

individual may be denied the right to participate in the decisions involving the political, economic, or social spheres of
communal life if others are permitted to participate. Each individual must be equally permitted to play a role in determining
the course of his life and the course of society as a whole. Other
individuals and social structures must not be allowed to make
or limit the scope of those decisions, or the ability of individuals to make such decisions, through the control of economic,
social, or governmental institutions. Thus, in this view, liberty
can be encroached upon not only by the state but by elites whose
concerns and desires are different from those of the greater mass
of citizens. The goal of democracies should be to alleviate all
encroachments on individual rights that are not necessary for
the greater social good.

The importance of the press in the democratic process has been
recognized since the seventeenth century. The need to permit
individuals to freely exchange ideas and information in order
to promote the public interest was regularly posited by democratic theorists. John Milton typified the idea in the mid-sev-
enteenth century when he argued against restricting ideas and
information, saying that truth should be allowed to grapple freely
with falsehood and that truth would ultimately emerge victo-
rious. Late in his life he described his view:

I wrote my Areopagitica, in order to deliver the press from the restraints with which it was encumbered, that the power of determining
what was true and what was false, what ought to be published and
what ought to be supressed, might no longer be entrusted to a few
illiterate and illiberal individuals, who refused their sanction to any work
which contained views or sentiments at all above the level of the vul-
gar superstition.[13]

This concept of the marketplace of ideas as a means of protecting public interests was accepted as a major tenet of Western society; but if the tenet is to operate effectively, the marketplace must be free of restrictions. That requirement has never
been realized, according to J. Herbert Altschull, who argues that
media are servants of power in all its forms and have never
shaken off restraints.[14] As the people's rights were protected

during the democratic revolutions, government restriction of the marketplace relaxed, but other restrictions were generally ignored and government restraints were never completely removed.

The restrictions on expression that Milton and his contemporaries attacked and that were addressed during the assertion and protection of individual liberties were put in place and maintained by rulers attempting to protect their monarchies by denying the literate population information and ideas that might reduce absolutism. Because the only significant limitations on expression were perceived to come from monarchs and their state apparatuses, attempts to protect expression during the democratic revolutions focused on government activities that limited expression.

At that time the marketplace of ideas was not subject to such significant economic controls as exist today, since it was not a fully commercialized field of endeavor on which writers and publishers depended for their livelihoods. Because the press was not yet a trade and only the beginnings of capitalism existed, the press was not as significantly controlled by publishers, advertisers, audiences, industrial structure, or the competitive economic system as it is now. Such economic and social restrictions were not foreseen as significant threats to freedom of expression at that time, and protections were not afforded against them.

The rise of mass society in the nineteenth century greatly changed the newspaper industries of Western nations. For most of their two-hundred-year history, newspapers had concentrated on fulfilling their political role and providing information that served the needs of aristocratic subscribers.

With the maturation of capitalism and the dawning of the industrial revolution, cities attracted large numbers of workers and rural towns began evolving into regional centers of commerce. The rise of mass production promoted the further development of advertising, as manufacturers promoted mass consumption in order to create markets for their goods. Urbanization made it possible for newspapers to break ties with aristocratic readers, who had previously been the only regular market for newspapers. With the rise and development of mass society and the development of technology for large-scale production, it was possible to produce a newspaper in sufficient quantity to sell at reduced prices and attract readers in the increasingly literate working population.

The manufacturers' use of the press as an outlet for commercial information led to great changes in the structure and operation of the medium. Publishers began shifting the burden of financing the paper from readers to advertisers, a development that provided advertisers great control over the content and distribution of the press because they provided most of the revenue as well as much of the content of the press. Publishers discovered that the rising amount of advertising turned newspapers into great profit-generating centers. They began to rely on the press as the major source of their income and writers became dependent upon the press for salaries.

These changes during the nineteenth century altered the nature of the marketplace of ideas by making the press's major role that of a marketplace of goods and services. Its role as a provider of information and ideas became secondary. The major marketing audience became advertisers rather than readers, and publishers began altering their content and reader demographics to appeal more vigorously to advertiser needs and wishes. The needs of the mass audience in democracies were submerged in the process, and the marketplace of ideas no longer functioned by allowing the public to make considered judgments about the worth of ideas. This marketing approach to information and audiences has lessened attention to ideas and their proponents and changed the way political information is presented, argues Dallas Smythe.

Our constitutional system originally rested on the procedure of submitting issues and policies to public *review, criticism* and *deliberative* choice between candidates. It assumed both rationality and free access of advocacy to the electorate. Cultural industry, by introducing a commodity view of politics, has gone far toward altering this system.[15]

These developments have altered the ideal of the marketplace of ideas in ways inconceivable when democratic theorists first sought to establish and protect freedom of expression. The commercialization of the press introduced new constraints on the marketplace of ideas and created a situation in which monopolization and concentration of ownership was inevitable. Subsequent professionalization of journalists and the emergence of the industrial press led to new definitions of news, new norms of ethics and propriety, new organizational policies, and new economic considerations. These changes have influenced editorial decisions about *what* information and ideas are disseminated, what topics are explored, and what questions are addressed. Similarly, *how* information and ideas are conveyed has been significantly altered. Most of these considerations are now stipulated by media owners and managers, professional organizations, and the social beliefs and values of reporters, editors, and owners, and by the structure of the industry itself.

Newspapers are now complex economic entities. As other media have rapidly developed and gained acceptance—especially since the Second World War—the financial stability of newspapers throughout the developed world has been threatened. Rising production and labor costs, changes in audience demographics and media use, and subsequent changes in advertising strategies and placement have contributed to rising newspaper mortality and a growing concentration of ownership.

This concept is the basis of the argument of this book. Choices in the marketplace may be removed by a number of factors and in a number of different ways. The limitation of expression and choice by any of the factors, however, subverts the possibility of truth emerging in the marketplace of ideas. It is unrealistic to presume that complete liberty in the marketplace is possible or has ever existed, because it is an ideal, but it is possible to try to establish a situation in which minority interests are not permitted to control the market for their narrow purposes at the expense of the greater mass of people and the public interest.

Some libertarians recognize the insufficiency of the view that only the state can restrict the market, but they do not accept the intervention of the state to correct the problem. The problem of economic control was noted by journalism educators Dennis Brown and John Merrill, who accept the libertarian viewpoint:

The enormously expensive technology of broadcasting, for example, can be operated at peak economic efficiency only when the very large audiences are being reached. Consequently there is a strong disposition to cater to accepted ideas and to shun the novel or the strange. This aversion to the controversial is by no means restricted to the electronic media. Many scholars in communication have noted a blandness which characterizes the mass communications industry as a whole—perhaps resulting from the commercial nature of its operation and the feeling that it is bad business to stray too far from convention. As a consequence, what is stale and accepted gets public exposure; but what is fresh and controversial often does not.[16]

Because the commercial nature of communication in the United States and many developed states creates a common denominator, a "reach-the-masses" syndrome, it is difficult to bring new ideas into the market. Information and ideas that may offend readers, viewers, or advertisers, or contradict accepted ideology or social norms, are subordinated, belittled, or—most often—ignored.

This commercialization of the press results in actions that control the marketplace, making it necessary to consider what has happened to the marketplace since it was described by Milton and, in the view of Western press critics, to take action to make the marketplace operate more freely once again. It is no longer enough to argue that those with viewpoints not carried in readily available media should seek out or start other media for those views.

With mailed subscriptions to major U.S. newspapers from another locality running as much as $300 a year (and providing substantially the same information as the local paper because of dependence on AP and UPI for national and international news), news magazine subscriptions reaching $50 a year, and subscriptions to journals of opinion and specialty magazines costing $12–15 per year, one could easily spend $1,000 a year seeking diversity. This kind of expense is well beyond the means of most individuals. And libraries no longer offer a ready answer to the problem, either. Government cutbacks have caused many of them to reduce periodical subscriptions at the expense of less-used serials, such as those with unorthodox viewpoints. Further, the inconvenience and time required to visit a library undoubtedly make the library an impractical source of day-to-day information for most people.

Starting competing newspapers or periodicals with significant distribution is out of the question because the costs of labor, distribution, printing, and editorial materials are so high. As one observer notes: "In a sprawling country like America, coverage in the mass media is the only means of gaining a day in the court of public opinion. . . . A mimeograph machine can't get the message across anymore."[17] Similar conditions exist in the other Western democracies, leading Jean Schwoebel of *Le Monde* to observe that "freedom of expression is given only to people who can assemble formidable capital."[18]

As broadcasting developed, it was argued that because of the limited number of channels available government should regulate the industry to ensure that diverse views and opinions could be introduced into the marketplace of ideas. The proponents of the view did not count on the commercial exploitation of the media, and the subsequent reduction in diversity of opinion. The argument for government involvement is still tenable, but one must also consider how to ameliorate the commercial nature of the industry. A similar rationale for government intervention has been applied to the newspaper industry today because the number of newspapers has declined to the point where the individual cannot easily receive diverse views and opinions, and thus cannot easily be an informed, active participant in democratic society.

In the United States, for instance, only 1,650 daily newspapers exist, and only 4 percent of cities served by these papers have more than one daily newspaper. The total number of newspapers has remained fairly stable in the United States, but the industry has seen high newspaper mortality in the cities since the Second World War. The loss of these papers has been offset, in raw numbers, by the development of suburban papers and small-town papers as population trends have changed, but noncompetitive markets are now the norm. The newspaper industries of European nations have not managed to stay even, however, and the aggregate number of daily newspapers has plummeted dramatically.

A major premise of Anglo-American libertarianism has been

that the transition from state market control to commercial market control ended press subservience to government and thus bolstered freedom. But economic developments in the press during the twentieth century—especially since the Second World War—have made it clear that the press can become subservient to market forces that also restrict freedom.

Among those interested in the contributions of newspapers to society, these developments have promoted concern that the press has abandoned its role in democratic society and has contributed to a decline in the prospects for democracy. As a result, a growing number of nations are studying, instituting, and increasing various types of state intervention in newspaper economics. These efforts are being made in hopes of bringing more stability to the newspaper industry and reducing the economic and social controls on the marketplace of ideas, thus promoting participation and diversity. State media policies are being increasingly discussed throughout the world, and constraints on the flow of information and ideas have become a major topic of discussion in United Nations forums.

This new intervention has not been confined to authoritarian countries or developing nations with marginal newspaper industries, but has also been instituted throughout the developed democratic world. Every developed Western nation now provides some aid to the press, in forms varying from postal rate concessions and exemptions from value-added taxes to subsidies for production and low-interest loans for expansion and modernization.

Although this intervention is intended to support democratic institutions, some people in the United States have seen it as an unwarranted intrusion arising from the prevailing philosophy favoring private ownership, economic efficiency, and accountability in the economic marketplace. Their view contrasts markedly with the philosophy, popular in most other Western nations, that the state must guard against the private abuse of economic power and seek to control the economic infrastructure of the press to ensure media plurality and the opportunity for a wide variety of political views to be disseminated. Yet even in the United States, efforts to increase intervention in press economics have had some success in recent decades.

Many libertarians have worried that the state intervention may lead to press acquiescence to, or over-cooperation with, government. Their distrust has not been unfounded, since there has been ample evidence that submission has accompanied government intervention in many nations, and that intervention has been used by some governments as a means of controlling the press. Although intervention may be benign or malignant, incidents of significant press control through state intervention have generally been confined to authoritarian or totalitarian states, or to nations without developed democratic governments. Evidence of press control in those nations, then, cannot be applied to democratic nations without serious reservations. In Western democratic nations where state assistance has been extended since the development of the independent press, the evidence indicates that intervention need not conflict with press freedom and that the traditional disapproving view of state intervention in press economics does not hold true in all situations.

During the past two decades, a variety of scholars, national study commissions, and international organizations have studied the effects of intervention in specific nations. They have explored the problems of mortality and concentration of ownership, the effects of various types of subsidies, advantages, and regulation upon industry structures, and the need for alteration and extension of intervention.[19] As a result of these studies, most governments have intervened in their newspaper industries in ways felt most conducive to public debate and exchange of ideas.

That intervention has increased in recent years indicates changing attitudes about the nature of press freedom and state-media relations in democratic societies. Many of these changes have been sparked by the democratic socialist movement in western Europe, which has led to a reevaluation of the role of the press and its importance in democratic society. One observer has noted,

The disintegration of a web of myths regarding the *freedom* of a market-based press and the inseparability of government subsidies and government interferences, coupled with increasing economic pressures on the press, is forcing media consumers, practitioners, critics, and scholars to rethink questions of control, management, funding, and ownership of the press.[20]

For the most part, however, the movement toward increased state intervention in the press has been ignored by U.S. media and by scholarly publications of the communication community, except for occasional criticisms based on traditional arguments against state aid. These arguments have not offered any substantive evidence that the potential dangers of intervention were being realized in the growing subsidization of the Western press. They have generally ignored the real issues behind state intervention or the significant intervention that already existed in the United States and other democratic nations. This is not to say that the condition of the press and the needs for intervention in the U.S. press have not been addressed. This discussion, however, has generally been carried on in relatively obscure journals of opinion and inquiry not usually associated with communication studies or public policy discussions.

With the exception of a few scholars and critics who approach the press from sociological, political, economic, and historical perspectives, the U.S. communication community has all but ignored the effects of existing policies on press organization and operation, the availability and allocation of information and ideas to members of society, and the ability of citizens to utilize communication structures to convey their views and wishes.

Studies of state-press relations here have virtually ignored the economic implications of public policies. Perhaps this is because, as one observer has noted,

communications markets seldom exhibit the characteristics for which theories appropriate to standardized commodity markets were designed. Not only are communications markets typically oligopolistic; they deal in services, often of a subtle and fugitive kind, and difficult to define.[21]

Although some discussions of public communication policy in the United States have attempted to show how public press policies restrict the use of capital and private property, few studies have concentrated on the manipulation of public policy by communication firms and industry associations to gain favorable advantages, subsidies, and regulations that protect and promote their interests. In Europe, however, reviews and criticism of the political economy of the press have preceded and succeeded the new intervention in the industry. New programs have been planned and existing programs modified in order to protect the public, rather than the private, interest.

This study explores the bases of such state intervention and its impact on public policy by focusing on the philosophical antecedents to modern intervention, showing how the rise and absorption of democratic and socialist ideals in the West has affected public policy discussions. The study postulates a democratic socialist theory of the press and discusses how state intervention in press economics—intervention promoted by democratic socialists—has been implemented in various democratic nations. It also explores the criticism and dangers of state subvention and regulation of the press industry. Various policy alternatives for advanced democracies are reviewed, and principles to guide press policy toward a less restricted marketplace of ideas are suggested.

NOTES

1. Robert Cirino, *Don't Blame the People* (New York: Vintage Books, 1971), 311.

2. Filippo Burzio, cited in Giovanni Sartori, *Democratic Theory* (New York: Praeger, 1965), 2.

3. See R. R. Palmer, *The Age of Democratic Revolution* (Princeton, N.J.: Princeton University Press, 1959), 3–24.

4. Leslie Lipson, *The Democratic Civilization* (New York: Oxford University Press, 1964), 517–554.

5. Sartori, 72–95.

6. Ibid., 252–261.

7. Robert A. Dahl, *A Preface to Democratic Theory* (Chicago: University of Chicago Press, 1956), 4–33.

8. Tocqueville early recognized the danger of minority repression. See Alexis de Tocqueville, *Democracy in America*, trans. Henry Reeve,

ed. Henry Steele Commager (New York: Oxford University Press, 1947), 156.

9. The problems and difficulties of democratizing public policy and remedies to those dilemmas are explored by Robert A. Dahl in *Dilemmas of Pluralist Democracy* (New Haven: Yale University Press, 1982).

10. See Thomas R. Dye, *Who's Running America* (Englewood Cliffs, N.J.: Prentice-Hall, 1976 and 1979); Thomas R. Dye and John W. Pickering, "Governmental and Corporate Elites: Convergence and Specialization," *Journal of Politics* (November 1974): 900–925; and G. William Domhoff, *The Higher Circles* (New York: Random House, 1970) and *The Powers That Be* (New York: Vintage Books, 1979).

11. For useful definitions of *freedom* and *liberty, democracy* and *democratic rule* and related terms, see such works as Thomas H. Green, *Lectures on the Principles of Political Obligation* (London: Longmans, Green and Co., 1931); J. Roland Pennock, *Democratic Political Theory* (Princeton, N.J.: Princeton University Press, 1979); and Robert A. Dahl, *A Preface to Democratic Theory* (Chicago: University of Chicago Press, 1956).

12. Giovanni Sartori, "Democracy," in David L. Sills, ed., *International Encyclopedia of the Social Sciences* (New York: Macmillan, 1968), 112–121.

13. John Milton, "The Second Defense of the People of England, 1654," in *Areopagitica and Of Education*, ed. George Sabine (Northbrook, Ill.: AHM Publishing, 1956), 105.

14. J. Herbert Altschull, *Agents of Power* (New York: Longman, 1984).

15. Dallas W. Smythe, "Time, Market and Space Factors in Communication Economics," *Journalism Quarterly* 39 (Winter 1962): 6.

16. Dennis Brown and John C. Merrill, "Regulatory Pluralism in the Press," *Freedom of Information Center Report* no. 5 (October 1965): 1.

17. Hazel Henderson, "Access to the Media: A Problem in Democracy," *Columbia Journalism Review* 8 (Spring 1969): 6.

18. Jean Schwoebel, "The Miracle 'Le Monde' Wrought," *Columbia Journalism Review* 9 (Summer 1970): 8–9.

19. The most important studies include individual national studies by the Commission of the European Communities, published in its Evolution of Concentration and Competition Series (Brussels: Commission of the European Communities); the 1972 report of the third Swedish press commission, *Reklam II: Beskrivning och Analys*, SOU 1972: 77; the 1972 Series Report in France, *Rapport du Groupe de Travail sur les Aides Publiques aux Entreprises de Presse* (Paris, July 1972); the 1976 report by the Royal Commission on the Press in the United Kingdom, Royal Commission on the Press, *Interim Report on the National Newspaper Industry* (London: Her Majesty's Stationery Office, March 1975);

Anthony Smith, "Subsidies and the Press in Europe," *Political and Economic Planning* vol. 43, no. 569 (1977): 1–113; J. W. Freiberg, *The French Press: Class, State and Ideology* (New York: Praeger, 1981); the 1981 report of the Royal Commission on Newspapers in Canada, *Report of the Royal Commission on Newspapers* (Hull, Quebec: Canadian Government Printing Centre, 1981); and Joseph Kaiser, *Press Planning: The State and Newspaper Publishing in Germany* (Zurich: International Press Institute, 1975).

20. Beverly James, "Economic Democracy and Restructuring the Press," *Journal of Communication Inquiry* 6 (Winter 1981): 119.

21. Dallas W. Smythe, "On the Political Economy of Communications," *Journalism Quarterly* 37 (Autumn 1969): 563.

2

Philosophical Bases of Democratic Socialist Press Theory

State intervention has reached a stage at which a new formulation is required for the traditional press ethic based upon a total separation of powers between authority and media. We can no longer pretend that information or media enterprises are utterly private enterprises existing at the convergence point of supply and demand.

—Anthony Smith[1]

The democratic socialist approach to the press has emerged in the past two decades. Social and political scientists in democratic nations have begun to view the evolving tenets of democratic socialism as a possible answer to government, economic, and social pressures on the press that control the content of messages carried and reduce the opportunity for diverse opinions and views to be disseminated. Consequently, citizens in many Western democratic nations have permitted their governments to intervene in the marketplace of ideas. They have allowed the governments to take a variety of steps to maintain and promote media and message plurality, to ensure press accountability to society, to provide public access to the press, and to open avenues for the public and journalists to participate in management decisions.

This concerted intervention in the previously sacrosanct realm of the press has been made primarily under the assumption that economic, political, and social forces have reduced and will continue to reduce the opportunity for diverse ideas and opinions to be introduced into the marketplace, a result threatening the very basis of democracy—informed citizen participation—unless governments intervene.

DEMOCRATIC SOCIALIST THEORY

Support for state intervention has grown rapidly in Europe, especially during the late 1960s and the 1970s. Many European governments have agreed to take action in support of a diverse press.[2] These actions include a wide variety of efforts, such as limitations on ownership, protective legislation, development support, exemptions from certain taxes, and the granting of subsidies that are consistent with the emergent democratic socialist theory of the press.

The theory departs from the traditional four theories of the press (authoritarian, libertarian, communist, and social responsibility) because it is based on sociopolitical theory and philosophy that has received its strongest articulation since the formulation of the four theories paradigm in 1956.[3] The democratic socialist theory is a theory for modern democratic societies. Although its strongest support has come in Western Europe, it need not be limited to Western societies in its application. It differs from the libertarian and social responsibility theories, however, because of fundamental differences in the view of the role of state vis-à-vis society. In traditional Anglo-American political sociology, on which the libertarian and social responsibility press theories are chiefly based, the state is viewed as the enemy of the people, and the word *state* itself has taken on a negative connotation.

In contrast, throughout most of the Western democratic world, the state is viewed as a more respected institution, pursuing policies on behalf of its citizens as a more openly democratic institution, and citizens and other institutions of society are generally supportive of that role. As a result, the state is not viewed with such great suspicion as in the United States. This is reflected in the political and social institutions and programs of such societies and in citizens' attitudes toward the roles of the press. These views have developed to the point where they can be articulated as the democratic socialist theory of the press, a theory that takes a very different—and much less suspicious—view of state involvement in communications than the existing Western theories.

This theory of the press has arisen concurrently with changes in Western thought and political participation during the last half-century that have led to a reevaluation of the roles of the individual, the state, and other institutions in modern democracies. What might be called a hybrid philosophy has developed out of this reconsideration of sociopolitical theories. The theory's hallmark is that it reasserts the democratic participation of individuals in all spheres of life that affect them.

The major impetus for this philosophy arose from the changing nature of the relationship between the state and economics, brought about to a great extent by the maturation of industrial-capitalist society. This relationship has increasingly denied citizens the ability to participate in economic and political decisions. Such developments as the growth of special interest groups and power elites, and the decline in opportunities to effectively voice opinions, have denied citizens the ability to participate fully in political, economic, and social decision making. As two political scientists recently observed:

The separation of economic and political power no longer exists. Widespread market failure has given rise, in this century, to the interventionist state. Routinely shaping, correcting, supplementing, and replacing the market mechanism, the interventionist state is explicitly committed to the task of economic decision making. But the expansion of state functions has not been accompanied by a comparably expanded system of popular participation in government. It had, rather, the opposite effect: political decisions have been displaced to an administrative apparatus that is detached from popular control.[4]

This occurrence in the United States has mirrored earlier developments in the industrialized democracies of Western Europe. There it spurred consideration of the emerging philosophy that combined the right of democratic participation in political, economic, and social spheres of life into a philosophy called democratic socialism (termed economic democracy by those in the United States who are specifically concerned with its economic aspects and by others who prefer to employ a description that does not include the often misrepresented and misunderstood word *socialist*).

Democratic socialist philosophy has had a great impact in Western Europe, particularly in the area of economic planning, and has brought about public planning and government intervention in many areas of economic life since the Second World War. Although the major parties in European nations now differ on the specifics of managing their economies, they agree that government should exercise wide control over the economic arena. In their view, "government must act as an economic manager, not just a referee. Instead of merely responding to crises, government should initiate action to ward off problems. It needs to assume greater responsibility for instituting comprehensive public policies."[5] The view of democratic participation in all areas of society arose mainly out of the works of theorists and critics in the highly industrialized Western democratic nations, such as the Federal Republic of Germany, Belgium and Sweden, and a few progressive, industrialized socialist states in Eastern Europe, such as Yugoslavia and Hungary.

Although discussions of democratic socialism are by no means new, no single volume has yet provided a comprehensive discussion of democratic socialist ideology or the role of the press in democratic societies operating with such ideology. However, a developing body of thought has begun to emerge during the past two decades, building on the turn-of-the-century works of early democratic socialists such as Eduard Bernstein[6] and Karl Kautsky.[7] Evan Durbin, who helped set the ideological tone for the British Labour Party, contributed a contemporary rationale of how socialism and democratic norms could be combined.[8] Historian Peter Gay noted the renewed interest in democratic socialism in the 1950s and explored Bernstein's impact on democratic socialist ideology in the first major American study, which pointed out the difficulty of trying to bring about radical social changes by democratic means.[9] In the last two decades Michael Harrington, founder of the Democratic Socialists of America, has been one of the most prolific writers on the subject in the United

States and has produced several books that deal with aspects of the philosophy,[10] as has Irving Howe.[11] Journals such as *democracy*, *Democratic Left*, *Dissent*, and *Socialist Review* have also carried articles that have contributed to the emerging view of democracy in all spheres of society.

The most significant contributions have emerged from the works on economics by an Australian political scientist, Carole Pateman,[12] and Yugoslavian economist Branko Horvat.[13] A variety of other writers have offered paradigms for putting the economic theory into practice; useful works have been written by Cornell University economist Jaroslav Vanek[14] and by Martin Carnoy and Derek Shearer, who authored a major work on economic democracy.[15] An introduction to this aspect of democratic socialism was recently published in *Journal of Communication Inquiry* by its editor, Beverly James, who broadly and inclusively defined economic democracy as

one element in the vision of a self-governing, self-managing society, a society in which the concept of democracy is extended to embrace all spheres of social life. Its fundamental aim is the construction of a more equitable and democratic society through the democratization of the economic sphere. The same rationale that supports the democratization of politics supports the democratization of economics: a humanistic belief in the inherent rights of all people to intimate, effective participation in major decisions affecting their lives.[16]

This democratic socialist view attempts to blend power elite and pluralist political theory with the class theory of society. This is accomplished by pointing out the debilitating effects of power elites and institutionalized interest groups on the democratic process, while at the same time drawing from the two theories' ideas and concepts that support classical democratic constructs—which have already been incorporated with class theory in the formation of basic democratic socialist ideology.[17] The democratic socialist view accepts from elite theory the view that elites dominate societies and institutions, including media and the state apparatuses. But it rejects the inevitability and necessity of elites dominating the state, concepts central to elite theory.

Democratic socialist ideology borrows the marketplace idea from pluralist theory and its rather pragmatic approach to reconciling the ideals of democracy with the realities of modern society. It rejects the view that changes in leadership or policy under pluralism necessarily represent real changes or the interests of the masses. It also rejects the view that individuals may not play a significant role in governing except through interest groups that represent various dominant viewpoints.

Democratic socialism borrows from democratic theory the concepts that each individual should play a role in determining the course of his or her life and the course society should take, and that other individuals should not be allowed to make those decisions through control of economics, the state, or other institutions of society. It firmly rejects the view that democracy should be limited to the political arena. Finally, democratic socialism borrows from class theory the basic concepts of class conflict and the idea that socialist economics and social theory would change societies from rule by the few to rule by the majority. Democratic socialism, however, rejects the ideal that only "pure" class theory can be followed, and takes into account historical changes since its introduction—particularly the development of middle classes—in stating its view of class struggle.

Such an amalgamation of philosophical and ideological concepts into a broadened ideology of democratic socialism is fraught with apparent contradictions, something that ideological purists in elite, pluralist, and class theory camps hasten to point out. Their criticisms focus on the fact that a pragmatic, activity-oriented ideology is created that does not dogmatically adhere to some of the rather rigid and, oftentimes, dated tenets of class, pluralist, elite, and classical democratic theory. Thus, democratic socialism is not only a hybrid theory drawn from widely diverse ideological viewpoints, but a major modification of the tenets of its "parents."

Democratic socialists, however, view their ideology as not merely a theoretical explanation of existing society and a vision of a more ideal and egalitarian state, but also as a plan for action—a strategy that recognizes the strengths and weaknesses of societies and the improbability of a revolutionary movement succeeding in advanced capitalist societies. The modern democratic socialist movement sees its blending of ideologies as a realistic view of life.

This view makes possible an evolutionary movement in advanced capitalist societies, a movement that can revolutionize politics and societies by promoting a fundamentally democratic society in which each individual equally shares in the decisions that affect all spheres of his or her life. This does not preclude the belief that revolutionary movements have their place and could bring about such a society in less democratic societies. In either case, democratic socialists seek to construct and maintain a society in which elites, institutionalized interest groups, and dominant classes give way to a single egalitarian class and a higher degree of democracy, a society that maintains some liberal values within a socialist system.

Democratic socialist theory, then, attempts to bridge the schism of political and social theory in modern societies. This schism was caused by the democratic revolution, which sought to endow man with equality, and the industrial-capitalist revolution, which moved away from equality through the development and maintenance of distinct social classes. These social classes, unknown in prior ages, are based on capital and employment.

Sociologist Tom Bottomore describes two stages of the democratic movement, a useful paradigm in explaining the aims of democratic socialists. The first stage was the revolution that brought on the concept of liberal democracy, a partial democracy that put in place a competitive political system that complemented the growing competitive market economy of developing capitalism. The second stage, he asserts, is the extension of democratic participation to other areas of social life.[18]

A weakness of liberal democracy is its limited scope, which generally permits the democracy to operate only in the political arena and does not extend to such areas as the economy or social life in general. This is the first stage of democracy in Bottomore's model, and adherents to a limited democratic philosophy seek to halt democracy's development here. They recognize that society may influence the state and should be able to alter it, but they reject the idea of the state being allowed to influence and alter society, even if the majority of citizens wish it to do so.

Democratic socialists take a much broader view of democracy, much closer to the classical doctrine. Economist Joseph Schumpeter describes democracy as a movement that tries to constantly extend the area within which the members of society participate fully in the governance of their lives.[19] This represents the second part of Bottomore's paradigm. Under democratic socialism, the state must seek to make it possible for the second stage of the democratic movement to succeed—the political and social dominance of the most numerous class, the working class, and the transformation of the market economy into a socialist economy.

Democratic socialists, however, are not statist in their approach to society and are critical of the centralized bureaucratic administration of economic, political, and other aspects of social life that is seen in most so-called socialist regimes in the world today. They are also critical of the state monopoly capitalist societies found in those Western nations that have pursued policies promoting centralization of decision making, bureaucratization, and regulation of society by the few. Instead of such types of "representative" governments—actually governments dominated by and skewed toward the interest of elites—democratic socialists favor governments that are not only of the people and for the people, but actually by the people.

Early in his life, Karl Marx supported the democratic revolution that was taking place in the Western world, but soon soured on the development because he saw that it was being limited to serve the interests of a few. Although he rejected the existing concept of democratic politics for a politics that sought to reconstruct political and economic society in a revolutionary manner, he did not reject the idea of democracy as the ultimate value for socialists. As one writer has pointed out:

Marx sees . . . a tension or contradiction between the principle of democracy—the full participation of all members of a society in regulating their communal life—and the limited, even distorted form which democracy assumes in a class society in which the bourgeoisie is dominant. For Marx, democracy is a historical phenomenon which is far from having unfolded all its possibilities, and the principle agent of its further development is the working-class movement.[20]

Bernstein, in his classic early statement on democratic socialism, points out the important ties of the working-class movement to the democratic movement, while revising Marx's class theory to take into account the growth of middle classes in industrial societies—a development Marx had not foreseen. Bernstein does not see this development of a middle class as a contradiction of Marx's analysis but merely as the creation of a new type of working class. He argues that the socialist movement was not based on a rejection of democracy but was a product of it: "Democracy is a condition of socialism to a much greater degree than is usually assumed, i.e., it is not only the means but also the substance."[21]

Peter Gay has correctly pointed out that the difficulties posed by an overriding belief in the democratic process and a belief that fundamental changes need to occur in society present a great dilemma to democratic socialists. This means that they are often forced to choose between following their principles, supporting the democratic process, and gaining their objectives very slowly, or rejecting principles, seizing power, and bringing about immediate changes.[22] In the Western world, democratic socialists have to date chosen principle over power and continue to work for change within existing democratic political institutions. Recently, Santiago Carrillo, former general secretary of the Communist party of Spain, underscored the view that democracy is an independent value and the objective of the working class.

As regards the political system established in Western Europe, based on representative political institutions—parliament, political and philosophical pluralism, the theory of the separation of powers, decentralization, human rights, etc.—that system is in essentials valid and it will be still more effective with a socialist, and not a capitalist, economic foundation. In each case it is a question of making that system still more democratic, of bringing power still closer to the people.[23]

DEMOCRATIC SOCIALISM AND THE PRESS

A major difficulty of participation in the democratic process in large societies is immediately evident when one turns to the press, which has become the major vehicle of public political information from elites and the major conveyance of political discussions and debates among elites. Increasing concern over the need to open avenues for public participation in such dis-

cussion and the need to reduce the power of existing commu-
nicators and media have resulted. Herbert Brucker has observed the need to change this situation:

In today's world of mass men and mass media, communication has
become so powerful that, ultimately, he who controls communication
controls the world. But communication is a power in a sense even
deeper than this. For no matter who uses it, or is used by it, communication in itself can be power, changing us as it washes over us.
    This means that our problem remains what it has always been: to
democratize communication. Journalism, and first of all print journalism, must fight not only those who use and misuse communication,
but, where need be, it must fight the mechanics of communication
themselves, just as in the past journalism has helped fight every other
tyranny over the mind of man.[24]

Mihailo Markovic has also argued the importance of opening
communication by removing constraints on ideas and opinions:

The genuine general will of the people can be formed only through
open communication, free expression of critical opinions, and dia-
logue. It is clear then, that any monopoly over the mass media (either
by big business, or the church, or the state, or the party) must be dis-
mantled. Such a monopoly enables a ruling elite to manipulate the rest
of the population, to create artificial needs, to impose its ideology, and
to construe its selfish particular interests as the general ones. Therefore the mass media must be free and genuinely socialized.[25]

The need to pursue such a democratic philosophy has been
pointed out by Edgar Friedenberg in his book *The Disposal of
Liberty and Other Industrial Wastes*: "The basic flaw in the democratic process is not that the average man is incapable of in-
telligent participation in the affairs of state. It is that he must
be rendered incapable of doing so in order to prevent him from
using his formal political powers to challenge the existing dis-
tributions of wealth and power."[26]
    The importance of media in carrying out that incapacitating
role has been pointed out by many critics, including Mattelart,
Siegelaub, Curran, and Schiller. Their views are typified by
Herbert Schiller, who recently warned, "The economic role of

the information and media industries and the services they provide . . . are now primary factors in the maintenance of the material system of power, domestically and internationally."[27] Beverly James has laid the groundwork for exploring means of democratizing the economic aspects of media, arguing that self-management and ownership are crucial to making the media more responsive to public needs.[28] Because serious exploration of media from the democratic socialist perspective has only recently begun, her work is useful in that it points out the needs and possible directions for future study.

More recently, James and Hanno Hardt have suggested economic democracy as a framework for redefining the nature of the press in Western societies. They argue that governments should strengthen weak newspapers and halt concentration of ownership, and that new types of newspaper ownership should be encouraged.[29] Vincent Mosco and Andrew Herman have recently argued that radical and neo-Marxist theories and research on capitalist societies provide methodology for analyzing the communication industry dialectically, and that they can provide ideas for democratizing communication in Western nations.[30]

Under the democratic socialist view, media can be truly democratic only if they are removed from the private sector, spared the effects of economic competition, freed from undue restraints and pressures—whatever the source—and induced to provide the capacity for citizens to communicate effectively with other citizens. These conditions include the requirements of the traditional Western liberal view of press freedom: the absence of government restraints and undue interference with communication of opinion and viewpoints. But the democratic socialist model also combines negative liberty characteristics (i.e., the absence of government restraint and interference) with positive liberty characteristics (i.e., action taken to promote a free exchange of ideas among all citizens, an idea that will be explored later in this chapter).

In the realm of communication, democratic socialists attempt to combine their hybrid political ideology with the communication theory of society. The latter theory was introduced in the United States in the 1920s by the "Chicago School," led by such

theorists as Charles Horton Cooley, Robert Park, and John
Dewey, who postulated that the rise of mass democratic politics was made possible by communication media that intri-
cately linked local communities to society as a whole.[31] More
recently, that theory has received renewed consideration by
members of the "Frankfurt School," made up of such critical
theorists as Leo Lowenthal, Theodor Adorno, and Jürgen Habermas. These theorists argue that communication media indeed played a significant role in the rise of politics and public
discourse, but that in recent years communication media have
been the cause of the decline of such mass politics and discourse. The reason for this decline is that economic and other
constraints placed on the media have eroded the prospects of
media being used to create a truly democratic society.[32]

Ed McLuskie recently addressed this problem, noting the rising support for viewing democracy

from a communication point of view; this means that democracy is
understood as a form of politics animated by and through general public
discourse, a politics whereby public discussion and debate are free to
make a difference. A necessary condition for the realization of such a
politics is that neither society, as a multitude of private interests, nor
the state, as the agency for public policy, systematically subordinates
general public discourse.[33]

To achieve such a condition would require changing the emphasis of communication from the use of media for one-way,
"down" communication from elites, economic interests, and so
on, to a two-way system based on what could be called "citi-
zen-communicators" and "citizen-receiver-communicators."

In a one-way system, such as that found in the United States,
media owners and managers determine what shall be conveyed with only a minimum of consultation with the audience.
Few real feedback mechanisms and little real public access to
the means of communication are provided. In a two-way system, the public has a much greater impact in determining what
is placed on the communication system, and institutions to
provide access to the media and means to respond to content
are provided. In the one-way flow situation, the audience is ba-

sically passive. In the two-way flow system, the audience participates actively in the communication process.

Commercial communication media and state-operated and controlled media, based on one-way information flow, are inimical to the interests of democracy because they inhibit two-way information flow, a basic necessity for the development and maintenance of democratic societies. Without the ability of citizens and groups to use media to freely voice their ideas, opinions, and concerns, democratic societies cannot survive, and further democratic development cannot be pursued because economic, political, and class elites are afforded the opportunity to control information and public discourse. Thus, elites can shape and direct the perceptions and opinions of the masses in ways that reduce diversity of ideas, tolerance of alternate opinions, and democratic participation in all aspects of society.

The modern ideal of individual political freedom and participation in the governance of society is only three centuries old. It has never remained a static program for democracy but has been continuously adapted to the environments in which it has operated. Democratic socialists believe that individual liberty is important and that such liberty must not be unduly limited by an institution of society. This ideology, however, departs from the traditional Anglo-American concepts of liberty in maintaining that an individual's liberty must be protected not only from state encroachment but from the encroachment of other individuals and of the economic and other institutions of society. Democratic socialists believe that the press is an important aspect of this individual liberty and that it must not be fettered if individuals are to have the opportunity to seek high degrees of self actualization and participation in society.

Forty years ago, George Bird and Frederick Merwin accurately pointed out the problems with media playing an important role in democracy: "Consideration of the press as a social institution forces the student of newspaper influence to face this paradox: the newspaper is cast in a dual role because it is both a private profit enterprise and a means of communication on which the public relies for social intelligence."[34] The democratic socialist view of media appears to be the first important attempt to rectify the problem of the competing media roles in

Western democratic societies. It works to ensure that media will help democracy operate at its highest level. Ljubomir Tadic points out the integral role media have to play in democratic socialist society: "An essential need of the workers' movement, therefore, is social criticism, which the proletariat rigorously applies to itself as well, in the form of self-criticism. In that sense, the role of the public, the widest political democracy, and freedom of initiative, assembly and the press becomes second nature in socialist society."[35]

Because media are viewed as a crucial institution of society, providing information and a forum for debate, it is understandable that democratizing the media should be a major goal for democratic societies. The importance of a truly free press has been recognized since the earliest days of socialist thought. Karl Marx himself acknowledged the importance of a free and vigorous press:

A free press is everywhere the open eye of the national spirit, the embodied confidence of the people in itself, the verbal bond that ties the individual to the state and the world, the incorporated culture which transforms material struggles into spiritual struggles and idealizes their crude materialized form. It is the heedless confession of a people before itself and confession, as is known, has liberating power. It is the spiritual mirror in which the people observe themselves, and self-observation is the first condition of wisdom. It is the spirit of the state which can be carried into every hut, cheaper than material gas. It is versatile, the most modern and all knowing. It is the ideal world which always originates in the real world and flows into it again, giving life, as an ever richer spirit.[36]

But Marx also recognized that such a free press was not without problems. "Bear in mind," Marx said, "that the advantages of freedom of the press cannot be enjoyed without toleration of its inconveniences. There are no roses without thorns."

ASPECTS OF LIBERTY

The liberal democratic definition of freedom of the press has traditionally incorporated two features—freedom to explore, review, and criticize the world in which the press exists, and freedom from government interference as the press carries out those activities. In 1947 the Hutchins Commission on Freedom of the Press recognized these two features of liberty. "Freedom of the press means freedom from and freedom for," it said, arguing that the press must be free from external compulsions and free to operate as an agent for the transmission of diverse ideas and as a surveyor of the world around it.[37] These two features adhere to the traditional libertarian views of the press's role and relationship to the state. But the Hutchins Commission went a step further, adding that the press has a responsibility to the society and must carry out its work in the best interest of the people, providing opportunity for diverse voices to be heard and public debates to take place.

Two divergent strains of philosophical thought on liberties are seen in the Hutchins Commission study. The idea of freedom from restraint emanates from the views of Thomas Hobbes and John Locke, and has been the guiding force behind the ideal of freedom of the press through three centuries of democratization in the Western world. The second concept—that freedom involves the liberty to achieve one's goals and that members and institutions of societies have responsibilities to their societies— rises out of the works of Jean-Jacques Rousseau and has received added attention in Western democratic societies since the Second World War.

The major difference in the two philosophical strains arises in the interpretation of how societies are formed and the place of the individual and institutions within society. Rousseau parted from the traditional liberal view in that he believed society is formed as an association for the common good and is guided by the general will. In his 1762 work *On the Social Contract* he argued that it is both just and proper to compel an individual to obey if his interests are different from the common interest expressed by the general will and his disobedience would interfere with the accomplishment of the goals of the general will.

In the 1950s, political philosopher Sir Isaiah Berlin began exploring the differences between Locke's and Rousseau's philosophies, and in a brilliant essay in 1958 placed them in the paradigm of negative and positive liberties.[38] Berlin described the negative sense of freedom as answering the question "What is

the area in which the subject—a person or group of persons—
is or should be left to do or be what he wants to do or be, without interference by other persons?" The positive aspect, he argued, is involved in the answer to the question "What, or who,
is the source of interference, that can determine someone to do,
or be, one thing rather than another? . . . Perhaps the chief
value for liberals of political—'positive'—rights, of participating
in the government, is as a means of protecting what they hold
to be an ultimate value, namely individual—'negative'—liberty."[39]

Reflecting on several decades of Berlin's work, Charles Taylor later explained:

Doctrines of positive freedom are concerned with a view of freedom
which involves essentially the exercising of control over one's life. . . .
By contrast, negative theories can rely simply on an opportunity-con-
cept, where being free is a matter of what we can do, or what it is
open to us to do whether or not we can do anything to exercise these
options.[40]

Under the traditional liberal view of politics, then, the state
has a dual function in democratic society. It must protect the
freedoms of members of the society from undue interference by
other members of society and by other societies and exigencies
that may reduce the members' freedoms. At the same time, the
state must keep itself—and be kept by members of the society—from interfering with freedoms in the society. Edgar Friedenberg has observed that this makes the state "both the guarantor of liberty and its enemy," because it must carry out both
positive and negative liberty functions.[41]

POSITIVE PRESS FREEDOM

Extending these arguments from the realm of individual liberty to institutional liberty has led to the concept of positive press
freedom, which combines the Rousseau-inspired aspect of liberty with discussions of freedom of the press. According to this
concept, society should promote conditions in which negative
freedoms may be exercised.

To Rousseau, morality lay in the priority of the people's interests; the community—i.e., the state—was the chief moralizing agency and the highest moral value because it protected those interests. Admittedly, Rousseau's ideal government was the city-state, not the large-scale nation-state, and thus his views are not completely transferable to large countries. His principle that some individual rights result in social inequities, and that these rights must be surrendered to the state if individuals are to be emancipated from the constrictions of social organization and the inequities of wealth distribution, has been accepted in socialist thought.

While Rousseau argued that the subordination of the citizen to the state was necessary to protect the public interest, he recognized the state's duty to be moral in exercising the rights it gained from its citizens through the creation of the social contract. In exchange for these new powers, the state must exercise the general will, provide liberty and material welfare, and remove gross inequities in the distribution of wealth. Any state not doing so would no longer be acting according to the general will, and thus have no moral claim to governance.

The democratic socialist approach to the organization of society draws from Rousseau's philosophy, but it does not maintain a statist view of society's future. Instead, it views state involvement in the direction of society only as a necessary vehicle for the creation of the democratic society. It seeks the achievement of conditions under which the "will of all" and the "general will" become synonomous and the strong state is no longer necessary for the achievement of liberty and equitable distribution of wealth and power. This approach is democratic, and its ideal is an equitable society in which citizens have the will, the capacity, and the ability to collectively make decisions that reflect the general will and the will of all. The highest moral value and moralizing agency in this society is the people themselves.

Rousseau, of course, was pessimistic about democracy. He believed that the collective opinion of the people, reached in their ordinary social roles, could be misled and thus lead to amoral governance. But, Rousseau argued, the general will—i.e., the universal concepts of justice, equality, and public in-

terest—will always be moral. One of the state's duties is to promote the general will in order to liberate the individual from
inequality, conflicts, and the injustices of civil society.

Robert Nisbet has observed:

The genius of the idea of the general will lies in its masterful utiliza-
tion of the ancient distinction between appearance and reality. We must,
Rousseau is saying, beware of the *apparent* will of the people, the will
that simple majority vote may make evident, for this is the will of the
people still incompletely emancipated from the private authorities and
the separate roles that are given them by history. The *real* will of the
people is the will that is latent in man and that requires as its condition man's liberation from these authorities and roles. *This* is the general will and is alone the "voice of God."[42]

Identification of the general will is not difficult under Rousseau's or the democratic socialists' views. The general will is the
equal distribution of power and wealth. Unequal distribution
creates social relations in which some individuals have advantages over others. Thus, when policy decisions are made to
promote equitable relations among citizens, the general will is
served.

Society, then, has a duty—through the state—to use legal and
social means to promote compliance with the general will among
deviant citizens. This compulsion is moral and proper if devi-
ance would harm the greater public interest. The development
of the idea that the state has a duty to protect citizens' interests
vis-à-vis the press reflects the evolutionary transition from the
traditional liberal conception of the role of the state to a conception of the state in modern democracies. According to the
latter conception, the state must play a supportive and subservient role to the democratic process, i.e., to the achievement of
liberty and equality in governance. Support for this view has
come from the strong Social Democratic and Socialist parties in
Western Europe and from democratic socialists in the United
States, since the view is important to their ideologies. In terms
of press-state relations, this has come to mean that freedom of
the press involves the free flow of diverse ideas and that the
state has a duty to promote conditions that allow and promote
this free flow.

Diversity is encouraged because it serves the ends of democratic participation and provides the means by which pursuit of the ideal democratic society can be undertaken in existing societies. Under a developed democratic socialist order, however, diversity would not be the ultimate goal and the state would not be a funder or guarantor of all vehicles for expression. Since its major goal is the realization of the general will, such a moral order would ultimately deny financial assistance to media that did not promote the general will and the achievement of governance by the people. After the achievement of such governance, this kind of society would promote only the voices of the general will and diverse views on public matters within the general will.

While seeking this form of governance, it is necessary to provide the means by which manifestations of the general will through the voices of citizens who make up the mass of society can be heard. This is accomplished by the promotion of negative and positive press freedoms. Ernest Mandel, an economist at the Free University of Brussels, describes negative freedom of the press as "the absence of legal and/or political prohibitions, the absence of censorship and of institutions a priori denying average citizens (or organizations of citizens) the opportunity of printing and diffusing their opinions." Positive freedom of the press, however, means "the effective material capacity of individuals to have their opinions printed and circulated."[43]

Efforts to promote positive freedom are seen in calls for social responsibility in the media, economic regulation, the right to reply, access to media, freedom of information, and state intervention in media economics, all concepts that conflict with the traditional liberal idea that government must not have a direct impact on media. Calls for positive press freedom are founded on the belief that the Miltonian idea that truth will ultimately triumph in the marketplace of ideas is no longer applicable because capitalist enterprises, which limit the introduction of concepts in conflict with their own, have "cornered the market." These commercial communication enterprises have brought about newspaper mortality and concentration of ownership through active pursuit of policies aimed at killing off their competitors and reducing the marketplace for ideas.

Gunther Nenning, editor of the Vienna paper *Forum* and editorial advisor to the Belgium-based International Federation of Journalists, warned about this development in the mid-1960s:

In the West today there is not a newspaper proprietor who does not kill his competitors. This is not only not prevented by state noninterference but positively encouraged. Under the noble but rather tattered banner of press freedom the press lords today slaughter one newspaper after the other. Today we have a state of war which calls not for noninterference but for the opposite: state protection against the murder of newspapers, state protection of press freedom.[44]

There is ample evidence that Nenning's assertions are valid and that the classical concept of negative press freedom has not only prevented state intervention from halting this "war" but has also led to government policies encouraging concentration of ownership and newspaper mortality.[45] Both developments have fueled powerful arguments that press freedom is being diminished, not enhanced, by unqualified support for the negative concept. In 1978 the Council of Europe's political affairs committee recognized this danger and warned that without public aid there would be a risk of the press in Europe falling prey to uncontrolled private interests, a result the council believed to be at least as dangerous as state intervention.[46]

Although the positive view of press freedom has been developing for the greater part of this century, particularly since World War II, it was not fully articulated until the last three decades. In 1953, J. B. Lieberman, a journalism professor at the University of California, explored the growing number of calls for freedom of information and access to media in the United States, pointing out their potential danger to the negative concept of press freedom. But, he noted, under the "heightened consciousness" of the positive purpose of the First Amendment, government could work to augment the press and the ways in which citizens receive information. He warned, however, that "every safeguard must be taken to insure that on the pretext or intent of augmenting the process, the actual result is not an intimidation or stifling of any individual or groups exercising the right to freedom of the press."[47]

Shortly thereafter, the authors of *Four Theories of the Press* noted that the recently articulated social responsibility theory was based on the positive liberty concept, but they did not postulate that positive liberty would become the basis of an additional theory of the press. It was not until a decade later that the idea of positive liberty was directly applied to freedom of the press. In 1966 Gunther Nenning applied the paradigm to journalism, extending the focus of Berlin's discussion of individual liberty directly to the institution of the press.[48]

Nenning argued that negative and positive freedom are not totally incompatible, saying that the traditional liberal negative view of freedom encompassed what the state should not do, and that the positive view included what the state should do to promote press freedom. "The old definition of press freedom is dying and the new one emerging. This agrees with calls on the state which are otherwise audible on all sides: the state should not be passive but take action—action to foster freedom by ensuring the conditions in which it can exist."[49]

Nenning's views were not widely disseminated and were never consciously accepted by American communication philosophers, probably because they evoked strong negative attitudes in supporters of the libertarian view of the press. Although the views were not circulated intact, some of the concepts emanating from the idea of positive liberty were used to promote government involvement, protection, and regulation of media throughout the democratic world.

John Merrill, in *The Imperative of Freedom*, briefly made one of the few journalistically oriented discussions of the positive concept. Merrill, perhaps the consummate libertarian in the academic mass communication community (Dr. Murilo Ramos of the University of Brasilia has dubbed him "the John Wayne of mass communication"), dismissed the concept—as would be expected—as "pseudo-libertarian," calling its proponents "elitist" and "utilitarians."[50] Despite Merrill's disapproval, the press in Western democratic societies has been guided by a utilitarian approach for nearly two centuries. During the early nineteenth century, James Mill, John Stuart Mill, the Society for the Diffusion of Useful Knowledge, and their followers were utilitarians in both the connotative and denotative senses. They pro-

moted a political view that played an important part in
developing the modern conceptions of the press and the state.
Though the Mills and their protégés differed on the ideas of ra-
tionalism and state control, they developed the foundations for
the notion that the press plays an important role in the relationship between citizen and state.

It has been observed that these utilitarians directed their ideas
at practical aims but that they "provided press reformers—
whatever the ultimate motive of those reformers might be—with
a coherent and forceful set of arguments."[51] Merrill, of course,
might argue that the neo-utilitarians are reformers with suspect
motives, but many others see purer motives, such as the attempt to preserve and increase ideological diversity in the press.

Media researchers and critics have noted the decline in the
number of diverse viewpoints appearing in the media. In the
U.S. press, for example, true diversity is absent even in newspapers that provide forums for the debate of ideas, since the
newspapers rarely provide the opportunity for views that fall
outside those held by the Democratic and Republican parties.[52]
Views on op-ed pages appear to be those of scholars, politicians, and others well within the mainstream, so the op-ed pages
should not be assumed to be a vehicle for views outside the
mainstream.

This development has prompted the charge that the "commercially based 'free market' of ideas is increasingly oligopolistic." "For all intents and purposes, the United States has no
opposition press. . . . Instead, as in any oligopolistic structure, the competition of ideas and commentary is limited to the
marginal differentiation of near-identical products."[53] Even let-
ter-to-the-editor columns do not provide significant access for
diverse views. Studies have revealed that individuals with the
strongest ties to the status quo and well-presented viewpoints
most often have letters published in those columns. "As it stands
now, it appears that one letter out of every ten mailed is printed,
with the percentage declining generally as the prestige of the
publication increases," Kenneth Starck, director of the School
of Journalism and Mass Communication at the University of
Iowa, has observed. "Those letters that are published seem to
represent majority views."[54]

Columnist and critic Nicholas von Hoffman has also noted

the limited views presented in the media and points out that "there are no Marxist newspaper writers in America, no avowedly socialist ones who are given space for their opinions; even the allowable liberals, and few they are, are twitchy-nosed, nervous Ivy League rabbits."[55] It may be added that anarchists, libertarians, and fascists also have difficulty gaining space to present their views. As long as that holds true, the press cannot truly claim to be a forum for diverse ideas and a bastion of democracy that deserves privilege and protection.

A. J. Liebling, the noted twentieth-century press critic, has observed that there is freedom of the press for those who own one, but that others do not have the opportunity to exercise the same freedom.[56] More recently, another proponent of extending freedom has argued, "It is up to Congress and the Courts to insure that the right to equal access and the right to hear all viewpoints are guaranteed, just as it is their job to insure people of equal justice, education, and the right to vote."[57] Herbert Brucker has observed:

The free press was not written into the Constitution for the benefit of million-circulation newspapers or multimillion-circulation magazines, still less for the broadcasting empires that can make the whole nation look at and listen to the same thing at the same time. The free press was established to articulate the yearnings of the individual, through a hand-operated press not unlike Gutenberg's.[58]

Professor Kaarle Nordenstreng of Finland, president of the International Organization of Journalists, expressed a similar concern:

(A) democracy cannot function properly unless there is original, critical thinking among its citizens. The realization of democracy is not possible if only dominant patterns of behavior and the pressure of public opinion offer content to people's views of the world. In such conditions one cannot speak of the will of the people, but of the people merely echoing the message put across by a small privileged group with control of both power and the channels of influence.[59]

Because of the problem of access for those who do not own presses or transmitters, and the need to protect smaller enterprises from larger ones, proponents of the positive theory of press freedom argue that its acceptance is needed. Despite warnings about the dangers of utilitarianism, positive measures are being enacted widely to ensure a modicum of freedom of the press in the Western world. These measures will be discussed in subsequent chapters.

Positive press freedom, then, can be described as supporting efforts that ensure the presence of conditions that promote the flow of diverse ideas and opinions. In order to encourage such conditions, it carries with it the specter of state intervention in press affairs. But positive press freedom is not a rejection of the negative concept that the state should not obstruct the expression of ideas and opinions or criticism of the state itself. Positive press freedom is an affirmation of that opinion process.

To supporters of the positive view, the term *press freedom* involves the combining of negative and positive liberty characteristics. It includes the relative absence of governmental and other restraints on the media and the presence of conditions needed to ensure the flow of diverse ideas and opinions. Supporters of the positive view hold that if either of the two aspects is lacking, social institutions must step in to develop them so that the press may carry out the roles and functions that make it indispensable to democracy.

This view presupposes that in democracies freedom of the press is a right of the people, not a privilege provided solely to those who own or control the means of transmitting information. Freedom of the press is viewed as an extension of the right of free expression, providing the people the ability to express their views fully without restraint from any elite. In the early stages of most democratic societies, the major enemy to such liberty is viewed as government, which has exercised considerable restraint of the press in the past. Not surprisingly, social and political philosophers such as Hobbes and Locke saw government as a threat to democratic society and supported the ideas of negative liberty, particularly in relation to the process of expression.

Proponents of positive press freedom now view Western society after more than two centuries of the liberal tradition and see new and rising dangers to the democratic process, dangers they consider every bit as threatening as an unsympathetic state. Rousseau argued that, in order to promote greater social interests, society may enter areas of liberty from which it normally separates itself. Supporters of positive press freedom, especially democratic socialists, extend this argument. They say that to ensure the means by which the democratic process of individual expression can operate, the state must step in to adjust the structure and economic systems of privately owned media, even if this means compelling the media to act against their wishes.

Yale law professor Thomas Emerson explains the view in this way:

In general, the government must affirmatively make available the opportunity for expression as well as protect it from encroachment. This means that positive measures must be taken to assure the ability to speak despite economic or other barriers. It also means that greater attention must be given to the right of the citizen to hear varying points of view and the right to have access to information upon which such points of view can be intelligently based. Thus, equally with the right and ability to speak, such an approach would stress the right to hear and the right to know.[60]

Positive press freedom is intended to promote the free flow of diverse ideas and public debate by removing and guarding against barriers to that flow. This is not intrinsically different from negative press freedom, which is intended to remove and protect against governmental barriers to the flow of diverse ideas and public discourse. Positive press freedom is not the antithesis of negative press freedom. Ensuring the presence of conditions necessary for expression to take place is not the opposite of prohibiting governmental restraint on expression. Both have the same purpose: to provide each individual the ability to express his or her view to other members of the society. Because this expression is viewed as a cornerstone of the democratic process, and because positive press freedom seeks to ensure the continued opportunity for that expression, the concept of positive press freedom could not easily be used to restrict expression of minority opinion in public matters.

Rousseau himself addressed the problem of compulsion, noting that it was not without limitations. "It is agreed that each person alienates through the social contract only that part of his power, goods, and freedom whose use matters to the community."[61] He also maintained that "the social contract established an equality between the citizens such that they all engage themselves under the same conditions and should all benefit from the same rights." As a result, he argued, those who limited the freedom of fellow citizens would also limit their own freedom. Thus, citizens would not hastily and thoughtlessly seek to reduce the freedoms of others.

Positive liberty can be used to reduce freedom of expression as it is currently practiced (i.e., freedom of expression made possible by wealth), but it can make possible real freedom of expression for the masses. It can be used as a vehicle to extend the ability to express one's views to the greater part of the population. Positive liberty could be used to reduce such freedom of expression only if society, expressing the "will of all" rather than the "general will," rejected democratic governance for an authoritarian form. Such a development is far less likely to occur than is the diminution of equality and expression now being fueled by unchecked capitalist control of the means of expression.

According to the positive press freedom philosophy embodied in the public policies of democratic socialists, media owners will be asked to give up some control over their "property" in the name of social advancement and the common good; the state will compel them to do so if they do not do so voluntarily. Although concern about asking the state to protect individual liberty and the democratic process is understandable, the state is the only institution capable of bringing private control of the means of expression into check. Short of complete social revolution, there is no instrument but the state to control the competitive forces that are rapidly diminishing the units of media—units necessary to carry the views and ideas of the public if the democratic process is to survive and flourish.

NOTES

1. Anthony Smith, "State Intervention and the Management of the Press," in J. Curran, ed., *The British Press: A Manifesto* (London: Macmillan, 1978), 72.

2. Since the early 1960s, and especially in the early 1970s, a large

number of government commissions have studied the economic problems of the press and recommended actions on its behalf. Most studies are unavailable in English, but they are available in the languages of the nations in which they originated.

3. The four theories became a standard in the U.S. academic communications community almost immediately after the press paradigm's publication. See Fred S. Siebert, Theodore Peterson, and Wilbur Schramm, *Four Theories of the Press* (Urbana, Ill.: University of Illinois Press, 1956).

4. Thomas Ferguson and Joel Rogers, "Oligopoly in the Idea Market," *The Nation* 233 (October 3, 1981): 303.

5. Charles Andrain, *Politics and Economic Policy in Western Democracies* (North Scituate, Mass.: Duxbury Press, 1980), 33.

6. Eduard Bernstein, *Evolutionary Socialism*, trans. Edith C. Harvey (New York: Schocken Books, 1961).

7. Karl Kautsky, *Das Erfurter Programm* (Stuttgart: J. H. W. Dietz, 1904). A collection of his writing is found in David Shub and Joseph Shaplen, eds., *Social Democracy versus Communism* (New York: Rand School Press, 1946).

8. Evan Durbin, *The Politics of Democratic Socialism* (London: Routledge and Kegan Paul, 1940).

9. Peter Gay, *The Dilemma of Democratic Socialism* (New York: Columbia University Press, 1952).

10. Especially useful are *Toward a Democratic Left* (New York: Macmillan, 1968); *The Twilight of Capitalism* (New York: Simon and Schuster, 1976); and *Decade of Decision: The Crisis of the American System* (New York: Simon and Schuster, 1980).

11. See *Steady Work: Essays in the Politics of Democratic Radicalism, 1953– 66* (New York: Harcourt, Brace and World, 1966); I. Howe, ed., *Twenty-Five Years of Dissent* (New York: Methuen, 1979); *The Radical Imagination: An Anthology from Dissent Magazine* (New York: New American Library, 1967); *Beyond the New Left* (New York: McCall Publishing Co., 1970); and I. Howe and M. Harrington, eds., *The Seventies: Problems and Proposals* (New York: Harper and Row, 1972).

12. Carole Pateman, *Participation and Democratic Theory* (Cambridge: Cambridge University Press, 1970).

13. Branko Horvat, Mihailo Markovic, and Rudi Supek, eds., *Self-Governing Socialism*, 2 vols. (White Plains, N.Y.: International Arts and Sciences Press, 1975).

14. Jaroslav Vanek, *The Participatory Economy: An Evolutionary Hypothesis and a Strategy for Development* (Ithaca, N.Y.: Cornell University Press, 1971), and *Self Management: Economic Liberation of Man* (Baltimore: Penguin, 1975).

15. Martin Carnoy and Derek Shearer, *Economic Democracy: The Challenge of the 1980s* (White Plains, N.Y.: M. E. Sharpe, 1980).

16. Beverly James, "Economic Democracy and Restructuring the Press," *Journal of Communication Inquiry* 6 (Winter 1981): 121.

17. The fundamental elements of the major approaches are outlined in Robert Alford, "Paradigms of the Relations between State and Society," in L. Linberg, ed., *Stress and Contradiction in Modern Capitalism* (Lexington, Mass.: Lexington Books, 1976).

18. Tom Bottomore, *Political Sociology* (New York: Harper and Row, 1979).

19. Joseph A. Schumpeter, *Capitalism, Socialism and Democracy*, 5th ed. (London: Allen and Unwin, 1976).

2C. Bottomore, 23.

21. Bernstein, 166.

22. Gay, ix–xi.

23. Santiago Carrillo, *Eurocommunism and the State* (Westport, Conn.: Lawrence Hill and Co., 1978), 105.

24. Herbert Brucker, *Communication Is Power* (New York: Oxford University Press, 1973), 228–229.

25. Mihailo Markovic, "Philosophical Foundations of the Idea of Self-Management," in Horvat et al., eds., *Self-Governing Socialism*, 331.

26. Edgar Z. Friedenberg, *The Disposal of Liberty and Other Industrial Wastes* (Garden City, N.Y.: Doubleday, 1975), 75.

27. Herbert Schiller, *Who Knows: Information in the Age of the Fortune 500* (Norwood, N.J.: Ablex Publishing Co., 1981), xv. For further examples of this view of media see Armand Mattelart, *Mass Media, Ideologies and the Revolutionary Movement* (Atlantic Highlands, N.J.: Humanities Press, 1980); Armand Mattelart and Seth Siegelaub, *Communication and Class Struggle*, 2 vols (New York: International General, 1979); and James Curran, "The Press as an Agency of Social Control: A Historical Perspective," in G. Boyce et al., eds., *Newspaper History*, 51–75.

28. Beverly James, "Economic Democracy and Restructuring the Press," *Journal of Communication Inquiry* 6 (Winter 1981): 119–129.

29. Hanno Hardt and Beverly James, "Newspapers and Western Democracies: Towards a Participatory Model of the Press" (Paper presented at the Sixth National Conference of the Society of Educators and Scholars, University of Illinois, Champaign-Urbana, October 1–2, 1981).

30. Vincent Mosco and Andrew Herman, "Radical Social Theory and the Communications Revolution," in Emile G. McAnany, Jorge Schnitman, and Noreene Janus, eds., *Communication and Social Structure* (New York: Praeger, 1981), 58–84.

31. John Dewey, *The Public and Its Problems* (New York: Henry Holt, 1927), 207–209, and *Democracy and Education* (New York: Macmillan, 1916), 3–7. See also Charles Horton Cooley, *Social Organization* (New York: Charles Scribner's Sons, 1925), 63–108.

32. For a general discussion of the Frankfurt School's view of media, see Nicholas Petryszak, "The Frankfurt School's Theory of Manipulation," *Journal of Communication* 27 (Summer 1977): 33–40. For a more specific view of communication and society, see Jürgen Habermas, *Communication and the Evolution of Society* (Boston: Beacon Press, 1978). See also Jürgen Habermas, *Strukturwandel der Öffentlichkeit* (Neuwied: Herman Luchterland Verlag, 1962). An English synopsis, trans. by Sara and Frank Lennox, is "The Public Sphere: An Encyclopedia Article (1964)" *New German Critique* 3 (Fall 1974): 49–55.

33. Ed McLuskie, "Systematic Constraints on Prospects for a Democratic Society: Basic Considerations from the Communication Theory of Society" (Paper presented at the Sixth National Conference of the Society of Educators and Scholars, University of Illinois, Champaign-Urbana, October 1–2, 1981).

34. George L. Bird and Frederick E. Merwin, eds., *The Newspaper and Society* (New York: Prentice-Hall, 1942), 77.

35. Ljubomir Tadic, "Order and Freedom," in Horvat et al., eds., *Self-Governing Socialism*, 414.

36. Karl Marx, *Rheinische Zeitung* no. 135 (May 15, 1842).

37. Commission on Freedom of the Press, *A Free and Responsible Press* (Chicago: University of Chicago Press, 1947), 18.

38. Isaiah Berlin, *Two Concepts of Liberty* (Oxford: Clarendon Press, 1958).

39. Ibid., 50.

40. Charles Taylor, "What's Wrong with Negative Liberty," in Alan Ryan, ed., *The Idea of Freedom: Essays in Honour of Isaiah Berlin* (Oxford: Oxford University Press, 1979), 177.

41. Friedenberg, 171.

42. Robert Nisbet, *The Social Philosophers* (New York: Thomas Crowell, 1973), 152.

43. Ernest Mandel, foreword to *The French Press: Class, State, and Ideology*, by J. W. Freiberg (New York: Praeger, 1981), vii, viii.

44. Gunther Nenning, "Negative and Positive Press Freedom," *IPI Report* (September 1969): 8.

45. The most telling recent example of this was in Oregon, where the Gannett Co. actively and successfully pursued marketing strategies designed to force its competition out of business. See Cassandra Tate, "Gannett in Salem: Protecting the Franchise; Court Documents Reveal Another Side of the Chain that Publicly Supports Openness and

a Diversity of Voices," *Columbia Journalism Review* 20 (July/August 1981): 51–56. Also see Ben Bagdikian, "Newspaper Mergers—The Final Phase," *Columbia Journalism Review* 15 (March/April 1977): 17–22, and U.S. Federal Trade Commission, Bureau of Competition, *Proceedings of the Symposium on Media Concentration: December 14 and 15, 1979*, 2 vols. (Washington, D.C.: U.S. Government Printing Office, 1980). The economic forces that have brought about mortality and concentration in the European press have been well documented in studies on individual nations published by the Commission of the European Communities in its Evolution of Concentration and Competition Series.

46. " 'Vulnerable'—That's the Press in Europe," *IPI Report* 27 (June 1978): 2.

47. J. Ben Lieberman, "Restating the Concept of Freedom of the Press," *Journalism Quarterly* 30 (Spring 1953): 137.

48. Nenning, 8.

49. Ibid.

50. John C. Merrill, *The Imperative of Freedom* (New York: Hastings House, 1974), 32.

51. Boyce et al., 22.

52. The development should not be surprising considering the narrow political view of editorial writers. A study of editorial writers' political leanings has found less than 3 percent to be outside the Democrat-Independent-Republican categories. See Cleveland Wilhoit and D. Drew, "A Profile of the Editorial Writer," *Masthead* (Fall 1971): 2–14. See also John Hulteng, *The Opinion Function: Editorial Writing and Interpretive Writing for the News Media* (New York: Harper and Row, 1973), and Robert Cirino, *Don't Blame the People* (New York: Vintage Books, 1971), 70, for discussions about the lack of diversity in opinion appearing in the media.

53. Ferguson and Rogers, 308.

54. Kenneth B. Starck, Jr., "Letter Columns: Access for Whom?" *Freedom of Information Center Report* no. 237 (February 1970): 5.

55. Nicholas von Hoffman, "Celebrating Mencken," *Saturday Review* (September 1980): 30.

56. A. J. Liebling, *The Press*, 2nd rev. ed. (New York: Ballantine Books, 1975), 15.

57. Cirino, 310.

58. Brucker, 212.

59. Kaarle Nordenstreng and Tapio Varis, "Television Traffic—A One-way Street?" *Reports and Papers on Mass Communication* no. 70 (1974): 7–60.

60. Thomas I. Emerson, *The System of Freedom of Expression* (New York: Hastings House, 1970), 629.

61. Jean-Jacques Rousseau, *On the Social Contract*, trans. Judith R. Masters, ed. Roger D. Masters (New York: St. Martin's Press, 1978), 62.

3

Models of State-Press Relations

The press lives—survives, rather—in an economic system that remains founded on profit; this leads to the concentration of ownership, and superficiality.

—*Le Monde*[1]

The liberal democratic ideal has been the dominant political determinant in the Western world, having been embraced by nearly every nation in Western Europe, the Nordic region, and North America. Since the earliest days of government by the people in these nations, the role of the press as a political educator and forum has been recognized and attempts have been made to protect the press from government pressures. Since the Second World War, however, new pressures have appeared—with devastating effects—that have bypassed protections afforded the press in the Western world. Newspaper mortality since the Second World War has reduced the total number of newspapers in Denmark by 51 percent, cut the French total by 49 percent, and cut the Swedish press by 39 percent (Table 3.1). Although the war years and reconstruction efforts altered the newspaper industries, the overall trend of newspaper mortality cannot be attributed to these factors alone. The number of papers has been reduced in every Western nation, although the loss has been less severe in a few countries. Great Britain and the United States, for example, have suffered newspaper mortality of less than 10 percent.[2]

Table 3.1
Percentage of Daily Newspaper Mortality since World War II

	Mortality Percentage
Austria	16
Belgium	50
Canada	0
Denmark	51
Finland	18
France	49
Germany	33
Iceland	0
Ireland	14
Italy	20
Netherlands	60
Norway	16
Sweden	39
Switzerland	20
United Kingdom	8
United States	6

Sources: Anthony Smith, "Subsidies and the Press in Europe," *Political and Economic Planning* 43, Report 569 (1977): 1–113. S. Hoyer, S. Hadenius, and L. Weibull, *The Politics and Economics of the Press: A Developmental Perspective* (Beverly Hills, Cal.: Sage Publications, 1975); and George T. Kurian, ed., *World Press Encyclopedia*, 2 vols. (New York: Facts on File, 1981).

Concentration of ownership among the remaining newspapers has increased dramatically, with newspaper chains and groups increasing throughout the Western world. Today, four firms control 40 percent of the total circulation in France, two newspaper groups control half of the circulation in the Netherlands, and a single firm controls 25 percent of the circulation in the Federal Republic of Germany.

A review of such concentration of ownership in the U.S. newspaper industry has led Patrick Parsons, a journalism professor at the Pennsylvania State University to conclude that the creation and maintenance of economies of scale in the newspaper industry are the primary causes of the decline of daily newspapers and of competing newspapers.[3] Parsons' work, which has received little notice, shows that newspapers operate in accordance with the primary functions, goals, and motivations of all industries in a capitalist free market system. Parsons also concludes that when faced with difficulties in the marketplace, papers make changes not to serve the community better, but to make the papers more salable. Such efforts are ultimately doomed to failure, according to Lars Engwall, a professor of business administration at the University of Uppsala, Sweden, who has argued that only by differing in content or audience can more than one newspaper survive in a given market.[4] Although Engwall's research has concentrated on the structure of newspaper markets in Sweden, it is relevant to those U.S. markets in which newspapers compete for advertisers and readers. The Commission of the European Communities has reached conclusions similar to Parsons', but it blames mortality also on new media that have changed previous advertising patterns and on changes in media use by audiences. The impact of these changes on national newspaper industries is documented in the commission's individual studies on press competition in European nations, published in the commission's Evolution of Concentration and Competition Series.

Neither mortality nor concentration of ownership is confined to the newspaper industry. Both can be seen in all industries in which individual enterprises are subject to the market forces of the capitalist economic system. A reality of this system is that maximum profits are not made in competition with other enterprises, but in the absence of competition. Because newspapers are, with rare exceptions, profit-making ventures—not public information utilities—it should not be surprising that capitalistic market strategies have spurred the decline of independent and competing newspapers.

These developments and the lack of mechanisms to improve message and communicator plurality have disrupted the forum of ideas in such a way that the introduction and debate of divergent opinions and ideas have been significantly impaired. This has prompted concern among political scientists, sociologists, journalists, and others interested in the contributions of newspapers to society and to the political process. The importance of newspapers in the sociopolitical process has long been recognized, and the effects of mortality and concentration scrutinized. It has been shown that political knowledge is influenced by the levels of coverage the media bestow on political issues and ideas,[5] and that media monopolies can strongly influence political attitudes and action. It has also been shown that "a public served by a monopoly is substantially less inclined to seek access to diverse media channels coming in from outside the community than is one served by competing media."[6]

These changes in the use of the press by audiences and press owners have turned the press into something that cannot be explained appropriately in the accepted theories of the press, and the existing Western-oriented theories are so deterministic that they do not permit significant public responses to these developments. Admittedly, no well-established sets of theory involving the press have evolved during the twentieth century, but it has been agreed that media are social systems that are shaped by the sociocultural context in which they exist and that they are closely linked to the larger society. Much of what has been suggested as theory has arisen from the heuristic emphasis of communication research. Many conflicting hypotheses and explanations have been offered, but little empirical evidence has been forthcoming to support the explanations. The study of the relationship between the press and the state exemplifies the problem. It has concentrated on normative models of the relationship, which often do not conform to social, political or economic reality. Since these models offer little pure theory, little prediction and almost no empirical testing of the models is possible.

For a quarter of a century, however, the dominant paradigm in the United States for defining and studying the relationship between the state and the press has been the one presented in *Four Theories of the Press*.[7] This book asserts that the relationships of states and media throughout the world can be explained by the libertarian, authoritarian, Soviet/communist, and social responsibility theories. In recent years criticism of these categories has arisen because they do not take into account political and economic conditions that exist in much of the world, especially in developing countries. The categories are also not well enough defined to account for the realities in much of the developed democratic world.

These problems are not surprising, since the model was developed during the Cold War. The three U.S. researchers who explored state-press relations were biased toward the liberal democratic tradition and its Anglo-American evolution. Their work thus favored the Western-oriented theories—i.e., the libertarian and social responsibility approaches—and disfavored the authoritarian and Soviet/communist theories. Although the beginnings of the nonaligned and nationalist movements were clearly visible in the Third World when Siebert, Peterson, and Schramm wrote their seminal work, the three researchers generally ignored the Third World—perhaps because they still viewed it as predominantly colonial or territorial possessions of First World nations. Even the most cursory review of the theories reveals the difficulties posed by the model today.

The accepted theories of state-press relations can be simply explained because they are rather simplistically described—a difficulty often encountered with normative models in the social sciences. The authoritarian theory emphasizes the absolute right of ruling monarchs or governments to use and control the press to maintain power and social stability; it is practiced only in some nations in Latin America, Africa, and Asia with strong governments headed by dictators and monarchs. But all nations—even in the "democratic" West—control their press in order to maintain power and social stability when those elements are seriously threatened by war or severe internal disorder. At other times the governments use subtle controls and manipulation. The communist theory asserts that the press is a tool for the party or government to use for social improvement and other policy objectives; it is practiced predominantly in Eastern Europe, China, and a few communist nations in the Third World. The libertarian theory places a purportedly unrepressed, privately owned press in opposition to government,

and the social responsibility approach champions a self-regu-
lating, privately controlled press with the same purpose. These
are found mainly in Western nations or other advanced democratic nations fashioned on Western ideologies.

Most developing nations do not reflect any of the four models,
since they are attempting to pursue state policies that combine
some elements of a relatively unrestricted press system with a
press system that enforces press responsibility and promotes
social goals. They must also cope with a dearth of media caused
by economic considerations that have kept private owners out
of the marketplace of ideas and information. The press policy
approach selected by such nations is clearly outside of the traditional four-theories model. Western attempts to enforce social accountability in the media, the proliferation of state-operated, supplemental media, and state support for private media
cannot be accommodated by the existing theories either and
point out the need to modify the existing model.

When the four-theories model was presented in 1956, it was
greeted as an interesting proposition, but widespread diffusion
and acceptance of the model did not occur until the 1960s. Even
then, however, the typology was subject to criticism. Most arguments focused on whether the theories represented actual
theory. Much of the debate was sparked by Siebert, Peterson,
and Schramm's articulation of the social responsibility theory,
which critics argued was only an observation of what the relationship between the press and state *could* be rather than an explanation of existing relations that would make it possible to
predict behavior. Even the authors were not certain the social
responsibility approach represented a theory. As late as 1969,
Wilbur Schramm called it a "premise," thus indicating the conflict surrounding the concept.[8]

Jan Robbins has noted the major criticism of the social responsibility approach. He argues that the approach is not really
different from the libertarian theory, but merely tempers the
philosophical assumptions of libertarianism by including allu-
sions to the personal obligations of classical liberal rights.[9]
Nevertheless, acceptance of the four-theories model became
nearly universal in the U.S. communication community by the
1970s. *Four Theories of the Press* became standard reading in

journalism programs across the United States, and nearly every mass media and communication philosophy text incorporated the paradigm within its covers, though the paradigm was only occasionally evaluated critically. One critic of the model has noted the widespread allegiance to the four-theories model and the difficulty of offering other views: "One doesn't blaspheme the trinity of Siebert, Peterson and Schramm in the presence of knee-jerk worshippers without risking their wrath."[10] The support garnered by the model can probably be attributed to the previously unrequited need for explanations of state-press relations and the desire to bolster communication studies with theoretical propositions—a particularly strong proclivity in emergent social science fields.

Despite nearly catholic acceptance of the four-theories paradigm, criticism mounted, and John Merrill proposed the first major modification in 1971. Merrill based his revision on the philosophy that there are really only two major approaches to state-press relations, authoritarian-tending and libertarian-tending, and that all governments are inclined to one or the other.

Men, as well as nations, tend to be authoritarian or libertarian. Of course, they are all somewhat schizophrenic, but basically they are disposed toward either a well-structured, disciplined world view with definite rules and an ordered society, or they are disposed toward an open, experimental, non-restrictive society with a minimum of rules and controls. Governments are designed on the philosophical base of one of these two basic orientations. . . . [11]

Merrill's view contained elements of Raymond Williams' view. Williams, writing in the United Kingdom in the mid-1960s, argued that communication systems involve not a simple choice between control and freedom, but "more often a choice between a measure of control and a measure of freedom."[12] Williams maintained, however, that three press systems could be found in the world: authoritarian, paternal, and commercial. Williams viewed all of them as subject to undemocratic controls. He proposed that a new system, a "democratic" system, should be the goal of public policy; such a system could be based on the rights to transmit and receive communications, and it could include protections against undue minority and majority control. Although Williams identified a few reforms in some media operations, he argued that no truly democratic press system existed in the world.

Ralph Lowenstein proposed a model that included the traditional authoritarian and libertarian theories; but he added a social centralist theory to account for communist and developing world approaches, and a social libertarian theory to replace the social responsibility approach. By 1979, he had modified his paradigm to call the Soviet model the social authoritarian approach and included the social centralist theory with the social libertarian model as replacements for the social responsibility theory.[13] While Lowenstein's modifications better approximated the realities of the modern world, they were never widely accepted—perhaps because the social centralist theory (later the social authoritarian theory) did not appear broad enough to cover all communist and developing world approaches to press policy. His major contributions, however, were the argument that the four theories lacked flexibility for description and analysis of all nations.

By 1980, the rapid expansion of independent nations in the developing world and increasing problems and state intervention in press affairs in the Western world had underscored the inadequacies of the four press theories and the need to alter the model. Clyde Slade asserted that the social responsibility approach, which depended on press self-restraint, seemed ready to evolve into a new press theory stressing social accountability and official action to enforce it.[14] In his U.S.-oriented criticism of the corporate press, Slade said the public might soon force government to act against the press to ensure that social needs were met. "Corporate newspapers stand at the crossroads. They can either choose to change to meet society's needs or await the consequences as society forces them to return to a status of social significance. They can no longer maintain the status quo."[15]

William Hachten shortly thereafter postulated a replacement model for the four-theories approach, and his typology offers a more realistic view of the existing world and state relations with the press. In his paradigm, Hachten offers five political concepts of the press: authoritarian, communist, Western, revolutionary, and developmental.[16] The authoritarian and communist theories are borrowed from *Four Theories of the Press*, as is the Western theory that Hachten created by combining the libertarian and social responsibility approaches under a single heading. He argues that both concepts developed first in the West and represent two different—but particularly Western—points of view. Hachten then proposes the revolutionary and developmental theories, views of state-press relations that have been generally ignored in the past but are now necessary for any comprehensive discussion of the world press situation. The former covers the use of the press by revolutionary groups; the latter provides a theoretical perspective for the use of the media for developmental purposes.

Under the revolutionary theory, the press operates outside traditional state-press relationships, supporting efforts to overthrow the existing government or free the state from foreign domination. This is clearly a transitional theory, one that is drawn from political reality and not from pure theory; it is operative only until the subversion it inspires is successful or fails. In the world of the 1980s, the revolutionary theory is seen mainly in the Third World. According to Hachten: "The revolutionary press is a press of people who believe strongly that the government they live under does not serve their interests and should be overthrown. They owe the government no loyalty."[17]

The dominant successor to the revolutionary press theory of modern nationalist and political independence movements is the developmental theory of the press. Its theoretical foundations are a combination of socialist thought and development principles, particularly the principles of utilizing communication media to promote development, as Daniel Lerner, Lucien Pye, Wilbur Schramm, and others have suggested. Under this theory, media are used to promote social and economic development and to achieve national integration. As Hachten explains, "The developmental concept is a view of mass communication from the many nations of the Third World where most people are colored, poor, ill-nourished, and illiterate, and it reflects resentments against the West where people are mainly Cauca-

sians . . . affluent, and literate."[18] Like the revolutionary theory, this developmental theory of the press is probably
transitional, but it remains operative longer. Nations practicing
this form of state-press relations may tend either toward libertarianism or authoritarianism.

Until recently, both the United States and the European nations were presumed to be operating under the libertarian and
social responsibility approaches. However, the increasing mortality and the concentration of ownership in the newspaper industry in the United States and increasing state intervention in
press economics in European nations have prompted reconsideration of state-press relations. Out of this reconsideration has
deveoloped the recognition that the libertarian and social responsibility theories have failed to provide answers to the
problems posed by increasing economic and elite control of the
marketplace for ideas, or to take account of the responses made
to such problems by a number of European nations, particularly those in Scandinavia.

In response to these types of concerns, two distinct bodies of
thought have emerged. The first reflects the traditional liberal
democratic view, joined with the capitalist, free-enterprise,
economic philosophy. It holds that the problems of the press
are unfortunate but argues that government must still be prohibited from regulation or from any other involvement in the
industry if any freedom is to be preserved. The second view is
more socially oriented, placing greater significance on preserving diversity of ideas and allowing government to take action
aimed at preserving and promoting the role of the press in the
democratic process.

Which of the two views a person accepts depends upon the
person's perspective, say Graham Murdock and Peter Golding.

The key question becomes one of public intervention or not. The argument is unavoidably political. On one hand the free flow of market
forces is viewed as the most justifiable influence on the range and nature of news and views made available by the press. On the other hand,
such forces are seen as a simple reflection of the distribution of power
in society—a distribution which the press therefore comes to represent
and thus to enforce. If this distribution of power is seen as unjust, then

so are its consequences, and public and state intervention in the affairs of the press becomes a necessary course of action to rectify such injustice. Which of these views seems correct depends on how one reads the history of the press.[19]

The interventionistic view has emerged from democratic socialist ideology, which developed in Western Europe at the turn of the century and was absorbed into the ideologies of the Social Democratic and Socialist parties there. It has been revitalized and has begun spreading throughout the democratic world in the decades since the Second World War. While the effects of democratic socialist ideology on European politics have been recognized, the ideology's impact on views of state-press relations has been overlooked. Democratic socialist ideology clearly represents another theory of the press, a view distinctly different from those identified by previous authors.

Like the social responsibility theory, this democratic socialist theory of the press requires media to open avenues for expression of diverse ideas and opinions. But it goes further than the social responsibility theory because it views the private control of an institution vital to society as potentially damaging. The state must ameliorate this danger by instituting new forms of ownership, operation, and management of the media, as well as by intervening in the economics of the press. This is the step beyond the social responsibility theory that the Hutchins Commission predicted in the late 1940s and that Clyde Slade suggested was beginning to occur in the United States vis-à-vis social accountability in 1980.

Under the democratic socialist approach, the press's purposes are to provide an avenue for expression of the public's views and to fuel the political and social debates necessary for the continued development of democratic governance. Under such an approach, the state acts both to ensure the ability of citizens to use the press and to preserve and promote media plurality. Ultimately, ownership under such a system would be public and not-for-profit, through foundations, nonprofit corporations, journalist-operated cooperatives, and other collective organizations.

The democratic socialist theory of the press has been drawn

from suggestions for improving the press that have been offered by a wide variety of individuals with a wide range of ideological backgrounds. To form its philosophy and define its requirements, the theory incorporates libertarian, liberal, and
socialist views of press freedom and press requirements in
democratic society. While it draws its various aspects from a wide
range of Western viewpoints, it is a distinctly socialist approach when considered as a whole.

The democratic socialist theory offers a significantly different
view of the press from that of the traditional theories of the press.
Under democratic socialist theory, the media are not instruments for private owners—as they are under the libertarian and
social responsibility theories, and can be under the authoritarian theory; nor are they instruments of the state or party—as
they are under the Soviet/communist and authoritarian theories of the press. Instead, under democratic socialist theory,
media are viewed as instruments of the people, public utilities
through which the people's aspirations, ideas, praise and criticism of the state and society may be disseminated.

In its view of state-press relations, the democratic socialist
approach lies somewhere between the social responsibility approach and developmental theory. The approach is built upon
the view that society leans heavily upon media in its efforts to
meet social needs, and that the state should help ensure those
needs are met. When viewed in the context of models of state-
press relations, the democratic socialist approach takes a place
beside the libertarian and social responsibility approaches, under the Western theory suggested by William Hachten (Figure
3.1). The democratic socialist approach and the developmental
approach have similarities that should not go unnoticed, but the
democratic socialist approach is more closely related to the concepts of participatory democracy. While both approaches draw
some of their philosophy from socialist writers, the democratic
socialist approach more clearly favors pluralism as a means of
achieving its ultimate goals.

Both approaches are concerned with the direction of society,
but the developmental approach involves more clearly defined
short-term social goals. Major differences in the approaches are
seen at the operational end of the models. Under the demo-

Figure 3.1
Five Theories of the Press

	AUTHORITARIAN-TENDING		BALANCED OR INDETERMINATE TENDENCIES		LIBERTARIAN-TENDING		
					WESTERN		
	AUTHORITARIAN	COMMUNIST	REVOLUTIONARY	DEVELOPMENTAL	Democratic Socialist	Social Responsibility	Libertarian
Developed	In 16th and 17th Century England; practiced in modern dictatorships in Latin America and elsewhere	In the Soviet Union after 1917; currently found in Eastern Europe and the Communist nations	In the Soviet Union before 1917; in independence struggles of Third World, and wartime occupied nations	In 20th Century non-industrialized, non-communist nations of the Third World	In 20th Century Western Europe	In the United States in the 20th Century	Adopted in England after 1688 and in U.S.; influential in Western and pro-western states
Out of	Philosophy of absolute power of monarch, his government or both	Marxist-Leninist-Stalinist thought, with mixture of Hegelian and 19th Century Russian thought	Writings of Lenin and experiences of early nationalist movements and resistance movements	Marxist thought combined with communication-for-development views of Schramm, Lerner, and Pye	Modern Marxist thought combined with writings of classical liberal philosophers	Writing of W.E. Hocking, Commission on Freedom of the Press and practitioners, and media codes	Writings of Milton, Locke, Mill and philosophy of rationalism and natural rights
Chief Purpose	To support and advance the policies of the government in power; to service the state	To contribute to the success and continuance of the communist social system, especially party dictatorship	To overthrow existing national government or free the state from foreign dominance	To promote national integration and social and economic development	To provide avenues by which diverse opinions can be made public; to promote democracy in all social spheres including the economic	To inform, entertain, sell — but chiefly to raise conflict to the plane of discussion	To inform, entertain, sell — but mostly to help discover truth and check government
Who has the right to use media?	Whoever gets royal patent or similar permission	Loyal and orthodox party members	The people who oppose existing authority	Government has right to use for programs for the public good	All citizens	Everyone who has something to say	Anyone with economic means to do so
How are media controlled?	Government patents, guilds, licensing, sometimes censorship	Surveillance and economic or political action by government	Uncontrolled by government or existing society	Government and/or party control, and legal constraints	Collective management and legal constraints	Community opinion, consumer action, professional ethics	By "self-righting process of truth" in "free marketplace of ideas" and by courts
What is forbidden?	Criticism of political machinery and officials in power	Criticism of party objectives as distinguished from tactics	Not governed by official proscriptions on content	Challenge to authority; information that would damage efforts for progress	Undue interference with individual rights and other recognized social interests	Serious invasion of recognized private rights and vital social interests	Defamation, obscenity, indecency, wartime sedition
Ownership	Private or state	State or party	By revolutionary organizations, sometimes with expropriated equipment	Private or state; most often state	Public (non-state), non-profit, and private (at this time)	Private unless government has to take over to ensure public service	Chiefly private
Essential Differences	Instrument for effecting government policy, though not necessarily government-owned	State-or-party-owned, closely controlled media existing solely as arm of the state or party	Essentially a transitional theory	Information is a national resource to be used for development; societal concerns more important than individual concerns	Media must not be unduly controlled by government, economic, or social interests	Media must assume obligation of social responsibility; if they do not, someone must see that they do	Instrument for checking government and meeting other needs of society

This figure is adapted from Four Theories of the Press, with inclusions for the concepts suggested by Hachten, Merrill, and Picard.

cratic socialist approach, the media are operated for the citizens' use and for the protection of the citizens' social, economic, and political rights. The developmental theory concentrates on the state's use of the press for the public good and forbids challenges to authority and information that might harm development efforts.

If one reviews the five major theories and subordinated approaches presented here in light of Merrill's authoritarian-tending and libertarian-tending paradigm, it immediately becomes clear that Merrill's view must be modified to include a region in which the direction is not necessarily clear. This is necessary because the revolutionary and developmental concepts of the press can be either authoritarian- or libertarian-tending, depending upon the circumstances under which they are pursued, and movement between categories is not only possible but, indeed, occurs. The democratic socialist approach attempts to reach a balance point between the two tendencies that best meets social needs.

The revised model of state-press relations that I have suggested and the explanations of the various theories or approaches are outlined in Figure 3.1. I do not believe that the paradigm presented here is the final, definitive explanation of state-press relations, nor that the categories are absolute. Some nations may practice forms of state-press relations that combine elements of different categories, and in the future new categories may emerge as subordinate approaches to the five theories or as completely new theories. Although I disagree with John Merrill's negative assessment of democratic socialism (he calls it "democratic utilitarianism" but places it between freedom and enslavement, in a position equivalent to that of democratic capitalism), I agree with Merrill that nations do not remain static and that a nation's press system cannot be placed once and for all within an exclusive "pigeonhole" category.[20]

While change and movement between categories do occur, the categories still remain useful for cross-national comparisons. Change usually occurs slowly, and state-press relations can be observed and compared and a nation placed within a category or a subordinated approach at a given time. In a dynamic world, such a measure is the best one can expect.

NOTES

1. *Le Monde*, October 31, 1974.

2. S. Hoyer, S. Hadenius, and L. Weibull, *The Politics and Economics of the Press: A Developmental Perspective* (Beverly Hills, Calif.: Sage Publications, 1975).

3. Patrick Parsons, "Economics of the Newspaper Industry: A Marxian Analysis" (M.A. thesis, California State University, Northridge, 1978).

4. Lars Engwall, "Newspaper Concentration: A Case for Theories of Oligopoly," *Scandinavian Economic History Review* 29 (Fall 1981): 145–154.

5. Philip Palmgreen, "Mass Media Use and Political Knowledge," *Journalism Monographs* no. 61 (May 1979): 31.

6. American Institute for Political Communication, *Media Monopoly and Politics* (Washington: American Institute for Political Communication, 1973).

7. Fred S. Siebert, Theodore Peterson, and Wilbur Schramm, *Four Theories of the Press* (Urbana, Ill.: University of Illinois Press, 1956).

8. William L. Rivers and Wilbur Schramm, *Responsibility in Mass Communication*, rev. ed. (New York: Harper and Row, 1969), 429.

9. Jan C. Robbins, "The Paradox of Press Freedom: A Study of the British Experience," *Journalism Quarterly* 44 (Autumn 1967): 429.

10. Jack Haberstroh, "Should Fourth Press Theory Really Be Called 'Make-A-Buck,' " *Journalism Educator* (April 1972): 9.

11. John C. Merrill and Ralph Lowenstein, *Media, Messages and Men* (New York: David McKay, 1971), 175.

12. Raymond Williams, *Communications*, rev. ed. (New York: Barnes and Noble, 1967), 124.

13. John C. Merrill and Ralph Lowenstein, *Media, Messages and Men*, 2nd ed. (New York: Longman, 1979), 163–169.

14. Clyde M. Slade, "Daily Newspapers and Social Accountability," *Journal of Communication Inquiry* 5 (Winter 1980): 43–53.

15. Ibid., 49.

16. William Hachten, *The World News Prism: Changing Media, Clashing Ideologies* (Ames, Iowa: Iowa State University Press, 1981).

17. Ibid., 70.

18. Ibid., 74.

19. Graham Murdock and Peter Golding, "The Structure, Ownership and Control of the Press, 1914–76," in G. Boyce et al., eds., *Newspaper History* (Beverly Hills, Calif.: Sage Publications, 1978), 148.

20. John C. Merrill, *The Imperative of Freedom* (New York: Hastings House, 1974), 23–43.

4

The Democratic Needs of the Press

An alternate mode of production, circulation and reception in the field of communications can only come about if there is a collective appropriation of the media and the creation of a new relations of power, knowledge and information. Furthermore, to demystify the emphasis normally given to communication via the mass media, it is necessary to add that if people were genuinely able to express themselves and communicate among themselves through the channels of popular power, as a normal part of everyday life, there would certainly be less need for these mass media.

—Armand Mattelart[1]

The democratic socialist approach to the press requires the satisfaction of a hierarchy of needs in order for the highest degree of freedom to be attained. Fulfillment of the subordinate needs permits higher needs to emerge, and as a society develops toward more liberty and democratic participation, it becomes concerned with meeting the higher needs. Herbert Brucker has observed: "A republic in which the people are the ultimate source of power must strive constantly, in the face of inevitable change, to democratize its communications."[2]

The developmental process of press freedom is continuous. Societies must always strive to gain or maintain liberty and democratic participation, lest these diminish through neglect. When a society develops to a point where it is concerned with higher press freedom needs, unfavorable developments in the lower needs can strengthen or weaken liberty, since the emergence of each need depends upon satisfaction of lower needs. If any of these lower needs are reduced, the society must redirect its attention to the more basic needs again.

It must be admitted, however, that liberty cannot be attained and maintained with complete stability. Constantly changing political, social, and economic situations require adjustments, usually made after the fact, in order to protect liberty. This process can be seen in developments in Western nations since the Second World War. During this era, those concerned with the further maturation of press freedom worked to increase press freedom by promoting autonomy in the newsroom, public acces to media, and changes in media structures that would make them more democratic. As threats to the very existence of the press began to develop, however, attention was returned to the more basic questions of economic restraints and plurality of media units.

Thinking of press freedom needs in terms of a flight of steps helps illustrate the view (Figure 4.1). As one progresses up the staircase, a higher level of freedom is achieved and the citizens' ability to participate democratically in communication is asserted more effectively. Before one can be concerned with the ways in which economics, society, or government hamper press freedom, however, it seems obvious that the existence of viable media must be assured. The first step in this model, then, is that the necessary technology and equipment for publishing or broadcasting must exist and be available for use.

If this capability for production and distribution is present, then the second requirement—an audience that is capable of consuming the product—must be satisfied for media to be viable means of communication. In terms of the press, this means that enough people must be literate to make printed material an appropriate means of communication. In terms of broadcasting, it means that there must be enough receivers among the populace to make broadcasting an efficient communication medium.

Economics, of course, plays a major role in the very survival of a medium, and the relative absence of economic restraints is

Figure 4.1
Democratic Socialist Hierarchy of Press Freedom Needs

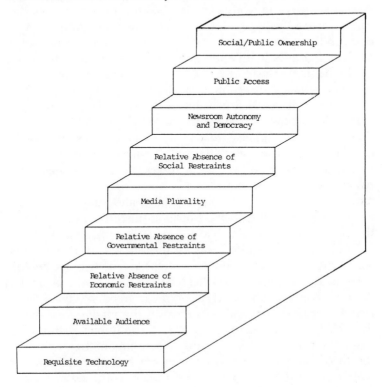

the third requirement. Without an adequate economic foundation—sufficient revenue from consumers, advertisers, outside sources, or some combination thereof—media cannot continue operating. Neither can they operate unfettered if they are forced to combat debilitating competitive forces that reduce the ability of some of a medium's units to survive. In 1978 the Council of Europe recognized all of this and recommended that governments take action to protect and support the media to ensure their survival.[3]

Two years later, the UNESCO International Commission for the Study of Communication Problems noted the decline in the number of newspapers throughout the world. It warned that increasing concentration of ownership and press mortality (both caused by economic factors) was limiting the variety of information sources and, consequently, the amount of messages they could carry.[4] Because of these and previous studies, many democratic nations in the Western world have intervened in media economics in an attempt to correct the instability caused by the damaging market forces of free enterprise capitalism.

This emphasis on economic restraints is the point at which the democratic socialist concept of the press begins to depart from those of the libertarian and social responsibility theories. The democratic socialist concept holds that under laissez-faire economic systems, the media come under the influence of advertisers, owners, and economic forces. These economic forces restrain and destroy the media because the media must ultimately lose their social consciousness and cater to the economic interests. This, in the Rousseau-inspired view, is not in the best interest of the public and must be ameliorated.

Once the basic requirements for the survival of media are assured, the next requirement for press freedom must be considered. It is the one most often cited in discussions of the traditional Western liberal view of press freedom: the relative absence of governmental restraints on the media. This means the absence of government-imposed conditions that unduly hamper citizens from expressing their opinions freely through the media and that hamper the media from providing information to citizens. This is negative liberty—the way in which government may not interfere—as distinguished from positive liberty—government interference that promotes liberties and democratic participation.

At this point proponents of the traditional Western liberal view of liberty generally end their discussion of press freedom, but those who take the broader view of press freedom under democratic socialist ideology continue developing the list of press freedom needs. Once the conditions discussed above have been met, press plurality (i.e., multiple press units) becomes the first need that must be fulfilled to provide the opportunity for diverse voices to be heard and ideas to circulate. Without such plurality, the number of voices that can be carried in the press is limited, as are the number of views about a particular event and the amount of information that units of each medium can carry.

Although unit plurality makes it possible for a large number of views and opinions to be communicated, the mere existence of media plurality does not ensure diversity. As Herbert Schiller has correctly pointed out, "What is most frequently presented as pluralism is, in most instances, merely another facet of the basic culture industry, organized commercially and anchored ideologically to private ownership and a way of life most conducive to its maintenance."[5] As a result, he says, what different units of a medium or different media present tends to be similar because the views of those who own or control the media are similar.

John Merrill has also observed that "a large number of media units can present very few viewpoints,"[6] but apparently he has not accepted the idea that such a development truly hampers democratic participation or the operation of the marketplace of ideas. Without media plurality, the potential for carrying more than a few relatively narrow viewpoints is severely limited. The democratic socialist model recognizes that message and communicator pluralism are also necessary for the marketplace to operate, and it provides for those elements at a higher level of the hierarchy of needs through access and autonomy provisions.

Placing media plurality after the relative absence of governmental restraints in this model reflects the view that government restraint places greater limits on press freedom than the lack of media plurality does. Although it may be possible to lack plurality, have no freedom from government restraints, and still have the distribution of diverse viewpoints, when there is media plurality and government restraint of viewpoints there is necessarily a lower level of liberty. But this is not to denigrate the importance of plurality in the attainment of a higher level of liberty, an importance recognized by the Press Commission of the Federal Republic of Germany when it said, "Freedom without choice between several alternatives is not true freedom."[7]

To climb to a higher degree of freedom, there must also be a relative absence of social pressures and restraints that may interfere with the expression of ideas and opinions or with the transmission of information. This type of restraint most often comes from pressure groups or special interest groups that attempt to shape information and editorial policies or to censor materials that they disagree with or find displeasing. The groups that bring about these social restraints usually include some of the following: 1) smut hunters—those seeking to halt the availability of materials they consider pornographic, obscene, or otherwise offensive to their sensibilities; 2) patriots—conservative political groups attempting to restrain dissemination of ideologies other than their own; 3) elitists—groups that believe themselves to be attempting to improve the quality of communication, such as groups working to improve television by suggesting and offering programming of what they consider to be higher quality or culture; and 4) minorities—groups seeking to improve coverage or images of themselves in the media.

When social restraints are removed or ameliorated, the seventh step in this press freedom hierarchy comes into focus. This requirement, newsroom autonomy and democracy, helps insulate journalists from the biasing influences of newspaper publishers and owners and the causes that they support. Several possibilities for this type of protection exist, including agreements between publishers and journalists or specific clauses in employment contracts with editors and other journalists. To date, this type of protection through joint control or cooperative management has developed mostly in Europe, through contractual agreements between owners, publishers, and journalists. A variety of publications offer varying degrees of protection to journalists, including *Le Monde* in Paris, *Dagens Nyheter* in Stockholm, and *Die Welt* in Hamburg. Such protection is almost unheard of in the United States. Brucker has explained the need and rationale for such protection:

None of us dreams of objecting to the fact that the local publisher, or the chief executive of a broadcasting network or multimedia complex, calls the editorial tune. By common consent editorial control is a right that goes with ownership. Still, once we begin to examine this assumption it turns out to be no different from that other assumption—

equally unchallenged in other days—that kings had a divine right to
rule. "The right divine of kings to govern wrong," Pope once called
it. We might call the journalistic version the publisher's divine right to
edit wrong. Whatever we call it, it is the right of money to edit.[8]

A study of reporter management has underscored what some
would term the shackled nature of journalists. "The journalist
is neither the free spirit of popular imagination nor the independent voice of democratic theory: he is a bureaucrat in an industrial society."[9] Jean Schwoebel of *Le Monde*, one of the first
papers to gain newsroom autonomy, has also noted the problem:

In the West, journalists are dependent on the owners or managers or
editors of newspapers or private radio or television stations. The men
generally do not permit their collaborators to write or say things that
do not somewhat correspond to their own ideas or feelings. Most of
them have uppermost in their mind the consideration of profit. Consequently they try to win and hold readers either by calming and re-
assuring them or by exciting them with huge alarmist headlines. Thus,
on the whole neither the government-controlled press of the East nor
the commercial press of the West genuinely serves the right of all citizens to be properly informed.[10]

The executive committee of the International Federation of
Journalists has recognized this problem and expressed support
for more reporter autonomy, saying it believes in "the need to
write internal press freedom clauses into new contracts and,
where practicable, to have such rights guaranteed by law."[11]
More recently, UNESCO's International Commission for the
Study of Communication Problems recommended:

Communication policy-makers should give far greater importance to
devising ways whereby the management of media could be democratized. . . . Such democratization of media needs the full support and
understanding of all those working in them, and this process should
lead to their having a more active role in editorial policy and management.[12]

The democratic socialist model also includes the concept of
public access to the press. According to this concept, individ-

uals and groups should have the opportunity to be heard or to directly express their views without having them interpreted or put into stories by journalists who may not understand the issues involved or the individuals' positions. This access also makes possible the diversity of voices and the ability to reply to other messages that Jerome Barron,[13] Phil Jacklin,[14] and other access supporters have urged. The right of reply, accepted in theory if not in practice in many Western or Western-oriented countries, has been significantly discussed in the United States only since the Second World War, beginning with the work of the Commission on Freedom of the Press.[15]

The fifth step in this model of press freedom provides for media plurality, and the eighth step—public access—provides for message and communicator pluralism. Phil Jacklin has argued the importance of such pluralism:

A society is democratic to the extent that all its citizens have equal opportunity to influence the decision-making process. Clearly, communication is essential to this process—just as essential as voting itself. . . . The media must be regulated, not only to insure a competition of ideas, but so that all citizens have an equal opportunity to influence and shape this competition.[16]

A variety of groups have recognized the importance of providing access, including the U.S. National Commission on the Causes and Prevention of Violence, which in 1969 reported that existing channels for information and views must be made available to the public. "Unless the individual has access to formal channels of communication, it is almost impossible for him to have an impact."[17] The International Commission for the Study of Communication Problems also recommended that public access be provided to promote diversity:

Readers, listeners and viewers have generally been treated as passive receivers of information. Those in charge of the media should encourage their audiences to play a more active role in communication by allocating more newspaper space, or broadcasting time, for the views of individual members of the public or organized social groups.[18]

Removing the press from the private commercial sector is the final step in this democratic socialist model of press freedom. The alternative suggested is not state ownership but societal ownership—such as that seen in public broadcasting in many Western nations, ownership by journalists' cooperatives, or proprietorship by social or political groups. Brucker has suggested that such "nonprofit" schemes could be successfully pursued because they would change the profit-oriented base of the press:

The ideal of a democratized ownership of the press, with internal checks and balances designed to keep it headed toward public service, while yet keeping it economically viable, could also be practical. Ever more complete and informed reporting, rather than ever more dividends, would be its guiding star . . . profits would be plowed back into higher salaries and improved mechanical efficiency, instead of being drained off into private pockets.[19]

Mandel has suggested a plan under which large printing presses and newspapers would become societal property:

They would be run under the administration of an independent agency (in French, regie would be the most adequate concept), with strictly limited powers of a bookkeeping nature, and under severe constraints of workers' control and public access to the books. Any group of citizens, whether organized in political parties or not, would have such access [to newspapers] in proportion to the number of signatures submitted (or votes obtained in elections plus signatures submitted). This means that given limitations on existing equipment, a certain minimum of public support would be required for the right to run a daily paper, whereas a lower level of public support would give the right to run a weekly, a bi-weekly, or a monthly paper. Special pages in existing daily papers would in addition remain open for smaller groups of individuals to express themselves freely. Press runs would be periodically adjusted to actual sales. The drop of sales below a given ceiling would then lead to the transformation of the daily into a weekly; and an increase in sales beyond a given threshold would allow the editors of a weekly to publish a daily if they wished to do so. The sales price of all dailies and weeklies would be identical. Subsidies would originate from the profits of other fields of activity in the printing industry and from the public exchequer, since one is, after all, referring to a sector that can make a fundamental contribution to the maintenance of democratic freedom. Additional guarantees and constraints would be added to avoid abuses, corruption or undue state influence.[20]

The area of ownership and management alternatives is of particular interest to individuals exploring economic democracy within the media industry, and can be expected to receive significant study in the future.

Sixty years ago, in a work on the press and government, Lucy Maynard Salmon criticized absolute press freedom as an unreachable ideal:

Preceded by censorship and by regulation, followed by government control and press bureaus, publicity committees, and organized propaganda, freedom of the press seems reduced to a mere mathematical point. The conception of it has always been fluctuating, never stable. It has been limited in one country by government action, in another by vested wealth, in another by political parties; elsehwere it has been controlled by the Church, in another country by the ascendant industry, in another by chauvinism, and everywhere by authority. Reasonable limitations are put on it by laws against libel and fraud,—unreasonable limitations vary with every changing breeze. Freedom of the press is as unattainable as is freedom of the individual, and yet,—we still believe, and rightly, that a country's freedom is measured by the freedom accorded its press.[21]

Democratic socialists recognize the difficulty of attaining press freedom and individual liberty, but are committed to pursuing these goals and acting to increase such liberties whenever possible. The vision of press freedom presented in the model discussed in this chapter is, admittedly, utopian, and I am well aware of the improbability of utopian conditions becoming the reality. But successful efforts can be made to reduce controls on the press which do not serve the causes of individual liberty and democratic advancement. To reject a normative model, such as the one presented here, merely because it is utopian in character would be to accept nihilism and a dysteleological view of the nature of human life.

Support for actions proposed under the democratic socialist

theory of the press has grown rapidly since the 1960s. It may well increase rapidly as mortality and concentration of ownership continue to afflict the press in nations that have not hitherto adopted significant measures consistent with positive freedom.

ACCEPTANCE OF POSITIVE PRESS FREEDOM AND STATE AID

The concept of positive press freedom has become the base for a variety of plans to aid the press in carrying out its democratic functions. The initial acceptance came in the Nordic region, where the strongest ties between newspapers and political parties have existed for most of the history of newspapering. When economic conditions diminished the number of newspapers there, those conditions were immediately viewed as a threat to the political process, and multi-party efforts were begun to find solutions that were consistent with democratic ideals. The major proponents of new intervention were Social Democrats, Socialists, Communists and members of some centrist parties.

Similar conditions in other European nations sparked interest in the Nordic countries' attempts to promote conditions conducive to newspaper health, independence, and editorial diversity. After Sweden first accepted the concept of increased government assistance in the mid-1960s, other nations watched its experiments with various methods of aiding the press. Sweden introduced a variety of aid programs, including the provision of funds to political parties to support newspapers articulating their views, direct subsidies to secondary papers in competitive markets, loan programs for modernization of facilities and equipment, funds to organize cooperative printing facilities among small publishers, and funds to help establish new newspapers.[22]

By 1974, poor economic conditions for newspapers throughout Europe led to extensive discussion of state assistance in national and international forums. The Council of Europe explored the problems, considered means to combat them, and finally recommended that state assistance be considered in affected nations. "The existence of a large diversity of sources of news and views available to the general public is of capital importance," the council said in its resolution.[23] Georg Kahn-Ackermann, secretary general of the council, later told the International Press Institute:

Economic circumstances have led to a concentration of publishing houses for books and newspapers unknown in the last century. In many countries, minorities and single literary voices which have no chance of selling widely, no longer have the opportunity to express their opinions, and in many parts of the so-called free Western World the economic process of concentration has eliminated the element of competition which is, so far as mass media are concerned, essential for the functioning of democratic society.

   In our times governments have a responsibility to support and protect the necessary basic elements for the free flow of information which in smaller countries, and maybe even in big countries, might mean giving subsidies—even big subsidies—to enable a free competing press to survive.[24]

Deteriorating press conditions and the desire to promote diversity for the sake of democracy moved reticent nations to accept the council's conclusions. Today most Western democratic nations—in Europe and North America—provide forms of state assistance not previously granted, and all the nations there continue to provide support established earlier. In its 1980 report, the International Commission for the Study of Communication Problems noted this development:

Smaller newspapers and some parts of the "quality" or "specialized" press have experienced difficulties from a contraction of operations and size, which has led to limitations on the variety of information sources. This has induced many governments to examine the possibility of subsidies to help keep newspapers alive or to establish new ones . . . in monopoly circulation areas and to promote plurality and variety in general.[25]

It was not by accident that the first nations to accept state involvement in press economics were those with socialist traditions, and that other early supporters had political systems and parties that were socially oriented. One review of the new situation states:

Governments have taken over responsibility to secure a politically committed press, and have thus replaced the parties as the most active transaction partner in the political arena. . . . If not exactly a reversal of the liberal theory that truth shall prevail in the free marketplace of ideas, this situation contrasts markedly with the most prominent means to this end: that the press must remain economically independent and free of government intervention. While the liberal theory makes freedom of the press synonymous with freedom for publishers, this new socially oriented theory stresses the freedom of choice for readers.[26]

Efforts to aid the press take a variety of forms, although the most controversial—direct subsidies—has received the most notice. Other assistance under positive press freedom includes regulations such as those limiting chain ownership or exempting newspapers from regulations with which other industries must contend. Some nations have instituted tax policies and other policies that encourage the establishment of new media to replace those lost due to high newspaper mortality. Similar encouragement is being given to cooperative publishing ventures, such as central printing plants that are to be used by several newspapers. Public broadcasting is also setting an example by pursuing strategies for citizen access and debate of issues.

Ernest Mandel argues that such aid is necessary because no mass-circulation newspaper can be run profitably today if it is totally independent of outside financial contributions:

Any daily newspaper, whatever the wealth of its owner, that would want to cover costs by sales alone would have either to cut costs drastically (that is, the number of pages published) or to increase its sales price considerably. In either case the mass circulation would disappear. So a self-financing, mass circulation, daily paper has not only become difficult under the third technological revolution, it has become impossible. Daily mass-circulation newspapers can survive only if they receive subsidies from outside sources.[27]

Mandel rejects income from advertising as an answer. He believes it forces newspapers to place too much influence in the hands of those who purchase space and puts newspapers into competitive situations that bring on newspaper mortality and concentration of ownership. The alternative, he suggests, is state aid and ownership through nonprofit corporations and cooperatives.

Anthony Smith, who conducted a survey of the types of state assistance offered in Europe,[28] indicates that newspapers have been and remain the mainstay of political life in most countries, and that governments have intervened with the best of intentions to preserve that role.[29] A review of the effects of subsidies in Scandinavia in 1976 came to a similar conclusion. According to media researcher Einar Ostgaard, "The Scandinavian experiences so far seem to give no justification to claims that 'government subsidies to press' mean less press freedom."[30]

In a review of subsidies, University of Utah journalism professor Milton Hollstein reached a similar conclusion in 1978. "There appears to be no evidence that general and indirect subsidies have compromised the press."[31] He noted that some concern still existed about potential press freedom problems. Nevertheless, Hollstein concluded, "Because European newspapers have been finding life hard, the prospect of the government dole is less abhorrent than it was not long ago. Governments for their part are accepting responsibility for providing economic 'protection' for a free but floundering press."[32] Even Raymond Gastil, director of the comparative surveys of freedom for the politically conservative Freedom House, does not quarrel with all state assistance: "Some government subsidies to the media seem to be relatively innocuous."[33]

Support for the state playing a role in communication also exists in the United States, where some of the arguments for state intervention have previously been used to promote a number of reforms and bring about tax advantages, exemptions from regulations, and other assistance for the press. These arguments have also been used to advocate less monopolization, further diversity of ideas, and a more socially and politically active press. But with the recent conservative victories in the U.S. political arena, President Reagan's desire to limit government activities, reductions in funding for public broadcasting, and continuing efforts to deregulate broadcasting—particularly in the areas of programming, equal time requirements, and relicensing requirements—prospects for increased government involvement in communication appear considerably diminished. Before the age of Reaganomics and the purported New Federalism, however, Thomas Emerson wrote in his superb work on freedom of expression:

It seems inevitable that government subsidizing of private expression will grow as the public section of our national life expands and the private sector contracts. . . . The supplying of government funds to enable various groups to utilize radio and television is likely to expand. Even government subsidies of newspapers are being seriously proposed. These developments bring obvious dangers. But they also carry enormous potential. They could lead to spectacular results: An enormous increase in the diversity of the content of mass media, a significant growth of popular participation at the community level, and a general invigoration of the system of freedom of expression.[34]

More state assistance is needed to preserve and increase outlets for opinion in the United States, agrees Donald McDonald, editor of *The Center Magazine*. McDonald argues that the United States provides aid to industries, farms, and other enterprises because of their perceived importance to society, and that it would not be much different to provide aid for the press, which certainly is more important for preserving democratic society. According to McDonald, "The public interest would also be served by governmental subsidies of additional mass communication media to promote a freer and fuller flow of the information and ideas that animate a democratic society."[35]

More recently, Herbert Gans has proposed that a national endowment for news be organized. It would help existing publishers and broadcasters increase the sources and perspectives of news they disseminate and help fund the development of new media:

Since news is not merely a consumer product but a utility as well, I think that the federal government should supply at least some of the funds for multiperspectival news (news presenting and representing as many class and organizational perspectives as possible). However, this idea violates the long standing formal separation of press and state. There are some dangers in ending the separation . . . but there are some viable reasons that justify it.[36]

Although one cannot actually expect efforts to be made toward such goals in the United States at this time, the fact that the goals can be suggested and discussed by reflective members of society is evidence of the growing support for the concept of positive press freedom, or at least for a mixed economy in the communication industries.

Reagan administration policy is strongly supported by the large communication firms and the libertarians who see unavoidable economic and social damage in government media activities, even if these activities are openly aimed at preserving and promoting citizens' participation in the media. Widespread support for complete deregulation of broadcasting content has developed among broadcasters and newspaper publishers, and the two groups have used their vehicles of expression to promote their views widely. Their efforts are specifically directed at equal-time requirements and the fairness doctrine, two of the few existing avenues of access to broadcast media today. Suggestions that pages of newspapers be opened to the public by law or by purchases of space for alternative views have been met with charges that such efforts would restrict the right of newspaper owners and managers to decide how to use their private property and thus restrict freedom of the press. While it is true that such involvement would restrict the freedom of those with wealth and power who own the means of expression, it would also promote freedom of expression for the public.

The arguments for an unrestricted press, however, are apparently not receiving much support among the populace of the United States. The results of a two-year study, published in 1980 by the Public Agenda Foundation, indicate that the public is not sympathetic to efforts to deregulate broadcasting, and that it believes newspapers should be subject to fairness and equal-time regulations in order to promote diversity and fair presentation of issues and ideas. The study concluded:

The media and the public share a common goal—a diverse marketplace of ideas. There is, however, a major disagreement about the means to the desired end. For most leaders (business, political, and media), the marketplace of ideas is best achieved by insulating the media and the press from government control or interference. In contrast, the public believes that the government should act to ensure that diverse points of view will be heard.[37]

Critics have long pointed out the rising number of "First Amendment junkies" who scream "freedom of the press" whenever they perceive that other citizens or the government are about to take action against them. In 1953 one critic warned that the phrase *freedom of the press* had "become tainted—whether rightly or wrongly—as a platitudinous subterfuge by which some publishers seek to avoid legitimate governmental controls on a purely business level."[38]

More recently, economist R. H. Coase of the University of Chicago has argued the issue similarly, pointing out opposition to regulation of the marketplace of ideas. He concludes: "I do not believe that this distinction between the market for goods and the market for ideas is valid. There is no fundamental difference between these two markets, and, in deciding on public policy with regard to them, we need to take into account the same considerations." Although he believes the approach to all markets should be similar—i.e., to protect the consumer against dishonesty and to regulate monopolization of the market—Coase says that actual public policy involving each market could vary to take into account democratic needs.[39]

A. Stephen Boyan, Jr., a University of Maryland political scientist, argues that changes in the field of communication now necessitate government action to protect press freedom. Government policies of regulation—and nonregulation—have allowed conditions to develop that halt public access to media, particularly broadcast media:

The character of government action, procedural regulation of speech, was always permitted and sometimes required under the First Amendment. But this aspect has historically been largely unrecognized because the thrust of its development was directed against *government* interference with the "free competition of ideas." Today, while government must continue not to restrict the expression of ideas, it can enact a variety of procedures to enable those who have something to say to the public to be heard. When governmental action has estab-

lished patterns of use of a public forum which restricts the free communication of ideas, it *must* enact such procedures. A democratic society can tolerate no less.[40]

State assistance provided under the concept of positive press
freedom or the democratic socialist theory of the press is not a
panacea for the problems in the Western world, however. At
best it is a vehicle by which to maintain and promote media
plurality, and possibly public access. Besides the potential dangers to press freedom, state assistance presents difficulties that
need to be overcome for it to be truly effective in promoting
participation in the democratic process. The most difficult
problem stems from the fact that Western industrialized nations, even those operating under partial democratic socialist
ideology, tend to pursue media policies that serve the interests
of large communication firms. These firms support the maintenance of the status quo and the preservation of class-differentiated society. J. W. Freiberg has noted this to be the case with
state communication policies in France since the Second World
War.[41] Bruce Owen has reported a similar finding in the United
States: "Both in broadcasting and in newspaper publishing,
economic interests have been generally successful in directing
the course of government policy toward the protection of profits and the prevention of competition."[42]

The Federal Trade Commission recently heard a similar argument from University of California law professor Stephen
Barnett, who reported that monopoly laws favorable to large
media firms had been promoted by the communication industry and that government intervention on the industry's behalf
was not supportive of diversity and pluralism in the media.[43]
Because of the consistent growth of government involvement
in and protection of industry in general, including the information industry, media owners cannot credibly argue that all
government involvement with media violates freedom of
expression.

Setting up assistance programs that do not direct their regulatory and financial aid to those who *least* need it requires considerable thought and organization, and should be based on a
firm commitment to securing the positive press freedom goals

of media plurality and diversity of opinion. Without regulations to help direct funds to those who would not survive without them, more harm than good can be done. Because of France's experience, J. W. Freiberg warns about indiscriminate fiscal advantages and subsidies: "The small, independent enterprises need these extra funds to survive, while the large corporate press groups use the funds to expand their domination through further takeovers."[44]

Other problems arise from the costs of state intervention in communication. Vast resources may be required to preserve media outlets, establish new media, and promote the inclusion of new ideas and news in existing media. If these efforts are to be effective, it appears that governments must commit themselves to these expenditures for a long time, something many are reluctant to do in light of poor economies throughout the world. Further, the lack of automatic regulatory and aid distribution rules in some government loan and grant funds could cause problems, although nations such as Sweden are now moving to develop nondiscretionary rules similar to those used for their direct cash subsidies.

It must also be noted that media receiving public support may lose incentive to improve, although there is no evidence that this has occurred. Evidence indicates instead that aid has improved media. Finally, there is the problem of media dependence on government intervention. This is a difficult problem because state assistance has become an integral part of many marginal newspapers' finances in countries where aid is extended. However dangerous this development may be, it must be acknowledged that without the aid the papers would not continue—a development obviously more dangerous to the flow of diverse ideas than dependence on funds.

Individuals adhering to the traditional libertarian philosophy are understandably reluctant to permit government involvement with media. They believe that the state is not benevolent and that, given the least opportunity, it will seek to reduce expression and citizen participation in democracy. The fear that government pressure and control will diminish freedom of expression is not without basis. The same may be said of the fear that economic pressures and controls and pressures from special interest groups will diminish freedom of expression. Diminished freedom of expression from any of these causes is equally damaging and reduces the ability of citizens to seek self-determination through the democratic process.

To sit by idly arguing that government should not interfere in the press in order to preserve press freedom, while economics, pressure groups, and even newspaper owners actively destroy the basic requirements of press freedom, is counterproductive and leads to a continual loss of press freedom. Of all the institutions in society, it appears that only government has the ability to step into the breach and halt the loss of press freedom. Acceptance of state assistance obviously carries with it the danger of state interference with expression. But many dangers can be ameliorated through vigilance and through the creation of administrative rules, procedures, and operating policies that limit the role the state plays in decisions involving the extension of aid. Evidence from the European experience indicates that these devices have been somewhat successful in protecting the press against dangers of state involvement and that the actions taken have indeed helped preserve outlets for diverse viewpoints needed for the democratic process to operate.

Today, proponents of the democratic socialist theory accept press systems based on private ownership and operated for the purpose of making a profit, although democratic socialists eventually hope to remove media from private hands. Under positive press freedom, the state plays a more active role in the media, but even when it attempts to aid only truly needy media, it often preserves the existing competitive economic situation. Despite the apparently democratic arguments for present state intervention in the marketplace of ideas, such aid cannot be wholly praised and accepted by democratic socialists because it does not strike at the heart of the issue—private ownership of an essential institution of society. At best, current state intervention is a vehicle by which media plurality can be preserved and is a means of moving up the hierarchy of press freedom. This once again typifies the dilemma democratic socialists face because of their ideology of evolutionary, rather than revolutionary, change in democratic societies.

How one views the efforts to utilize the positive press freedom concept and to implement the democratic socialist theory of the press is inherently wrapped up in questions of political and social ideology. If one believes in an unfettered free enterprise system, and if one believes that only government can truly threaten press freedom, then the democratic socialist theory will be viewed as a severe restraint upon and interference with the marketplace. If one supports the social responsibility theory, the democratic socialist alternative will also be unpalatable because it puts even less faith in the idea that truth on its own will ultimately triumph in the commercial marketplace of ideas. An uncompromising socialist will likewise disapprove of positive press freedom and the new state intervention since the democratic socialist view does not require media to be immediately wrested from private hands.

The course that the majority of democratic socialists have selected is not surprising, however, because democratic socialism was first developed and implemented in nations pursuing state capitalism and "responsible" competitive strategies. The blending of ideologies into the new theory of the press can be viewed as a step in the direction of popular access to and control of the media, a development that may lead to true democratic ownership and operation of the means of disseminating information and opinion under democratic socialism.

NOTES

1. Armand Mattelart, *Mass Media, Ideologies and the Revolutionary Movement* (Atlantic Highlands, N.J.: Humanities Press, 1980), xiv–xv.

2. Herbert Brucker, *Communication Is Power* (New York: Oxford University Press, 1973), viii.

3. Council of Europe, Resolution 834 (1978).

4. International Commission for the Study of Communication Problems, *Many Voices, One World* (New York: Unipub, 1980).

5. Herbert I. Schiller, *Communication and Cultural Domination* (White Plains, N.Y.: M. E. Sharpe, 1976), 108.

6. John C. Merrill, *The Imperative of Freedom* (New York: Hastings House, 1974), 69–70.

7. Final Report of the Press Commission, June 14, 1968, BT Drucks V/3122, p. 13.

8. Brucker, 336.

9. James H. Bissland, "Reforming the Press: The Democratic Alternative to News Media Bureaucracy" (Ph.D. diss., University of Iowa, 1976), 1–2.

10. Jean Schwoebel, *Newsroom Democracy: The Case for Independence of the Press*, Iowa Center for Communication Study Monograph Series, no. 2 (Iowa City, Iowa: University of Iowa School of Journalism, 1976), 23.

11. David J. Hart, "Changing Relationships between Publishers and Journalists: An Overview," in Anthony Smith, ed., *Newspapers and Democracy* (Cambridge, Mass.: MIT Press, 1980), 271.

12. International Commission for the Study of Communication Problems, 267.

13. See "Access to the Press: A New First Amendment Right," *Harvard Law Review* 80 (June 1967): 1641, and *Freedom of the Press for Whom? The Rise of Access to Mass Media* (Bloomington, Ind.: Indiana University Press, 1973).

14. Phil Jacklin, "A New Fairness Doctrine: Access to the Media," *The Center Magazine* 8 (May/June 1975): 46–50.

15. In the late 1940s, the Hutchins Commission considered the issue and argued that a right to reply should be formulated in U.S. law. See Zachariah Chafee, Jr., *Government and Mass Communication*, 2 vols. (Chicago: University of Chicago Press, 1947), vol. 1, 145–199. The issue lay dormant until the 1970s, when the concept of the right to reply and to access to express public views was widely debated. The debate subsided again after the Supreme Court of the United States ruled (*Miami Herald Publishing Co. v. Tornillo*, 418 U.S. 241, 94 S. Ct. 2831, 41 L. Ed. 2nd 730) that there was no guarantee of access under the First Amendment and that a Florida statute providing candidates a right to reply to newspaper attacks violated the First Amendment.

16. Jacklin, 49.

17. National Commission on the Causes and Prevention of Violence, *Mass Media and Violence* (Washington, D.C.: U.S. Government Printing Office, 1969), 68.

18. International Commission for the Study of Communication Problems, 267.

19. Brucker, 353.

20. Ernest Mandel, foreword to J. W. Freiberg, *The French Press: Class, State, and Ideology* (New York: Praeger, 1981), xiii.

21. Lucy Maynard Salmon, *The Newspaper and Authority* (New York: Oxford University Press, 1923), 280.

22. Robert G. Picard, "State Aid and the Press: A Case Study of Newspapers in Two Swedish Cities, 1965–1978" (M.A. thesis, California State University, Fullerton, 1979), 63–82.

23. Council of Europe, Resolution 43 (1974) on Press Concentration.

24. Georg Kahn-Ackermann, "Hiding the Truth under Mountains of Facts," *IPI Report* 24 (July 1975): 4.

25. International Commission for the Study of Communication Problems, 101.

26. Hoyer, Hadenius, and Weibull, 57.

27. Mandel, xii.

28. Anthony Smith, "Subsidies and the Press in Europe," *Political and Economic Planning*, no. 569 (1977): 1–113.

29. Ibid., 13.

30. Einar Ostgaard, "Effects of Growing Dependence on Governmental Aid: Analysis of Official Reports Published in Norway and Sweden," *IPI Report* 25 (April 1976): 18.

31. Milton Hollstein, "Government and the Press: The Question of Subsidies," *Journal of Communication* 28 (Autumn 1978): 16.

32. Ibid., 15.

33. Raymond Gastil, personal letter, 14 May 1979.

34. Emerson, 652.

35. Donald McDonald, "The Media's Conflicts of Interest," *The Center Magazine* (November/December 1976): 16.

36. Herbert J. Gans, *Deciding What's News* (New York: Pantheon Books, 1979), 328.

37. Public Agenda Foundation, *The Speaker and the Listener* (New York: Public Agenda Foundation, 1980), 1: 15.

38. Lieberman, 131.

39. R. H. Coase, "The Economics of the First Amendment: The Market for Goods and the Market for Ideas," *American Economic Review* 64 (May 1974): 389.

40. A. Stephen Boyan, Jr., "The Ability to Communicate: A First Amendment Right," in Harry M. Clor, ed., *The Mass Media and Modern Democracy* (Chicago: Rand McNally College Publishing Co., 1974), 142.

41. J. W. Freiberg, *The French Press: Class, State, and Ideology* (New York: Praeger, 1981).

42. Bruce Owen, *Economics and Freedom of Expression: Media Structure and the First Amendment* (Cambridge, Mass.: Ballinger Publishing Co., 1975), 183.

43. Stephen E. Barnett, "Media Monopoly and the Law," *Journal of Communication* 30 (Spring 1980): 72–80.

44. Freiberg, 171.

5

Patterns and Types of Intervention

Despite the fact that many people feel that all kinds of state supports for the press are unnecessary, and even detrimental to free speech and to the freedom of the press, experience shows that—just as the state subsidizes other branches of the economy—a correctly structured system of support for the press may be necessary (depending on circumstances in each particular country) in order to ensure the continuing activity of the press and its variety and pluralism.

—Simopekka Nortamo[1]

FUNCTIONS OF INTERVENTION

Modern state intervention in press economics has generally been instituted in response to structural and economic problems in the industry. But states also have intervened to support the industry, as in the late nineteenth century, when newspapers asserted independence from government. State intervention in the private economy serves four purposes: 1) provision of facilities valuable to a specific industry or group of industries, such as railroads, ports, roads, communication, and power facilities that support production and distribution of goods and services; 2) investment in the economic infrastructure through educational spending, general business advantages, credit guarantees, and insurance programs that generally support the capitalist economic system; 3) expenditures to stabilize the political climate for profitable private investment, through redevelopment programs, medical payments, unemployment benefits, and anti-

poverty programs; and 4) foreign aid activities that benefit
commercial interests by stabilizing potential markets, developing new markets, and providing banking advantages, credit
schemes, and guarantee programs that subsidize the purchase
of products and services.[2]

In modern democratic societies the state also intervenes to
balance contradictory interests between different industrial sectors, to favor big capital over small capital in certain industries,
and to protect and extend the interests of the state (i.e., the bureaucracy).[3] But intervention need not always be active, according to J. W. Freiberg, who argues: "State intervention can be
passive as well as active. By *not* intervening, the state can choose
to favor certain interests over others."[4] In Western societies, the
state has traditionally intervened in media economics in four
areas: telecommunication regulation and support, supervision
of monopolization, provision of information on the processes
of government, and organization of political debate.[5]

Despite widespread intervention in economics in all modern
industrial states, some observers in Western democratic nations remain uneasy about government involvement in the economic sphere. This is particularly true in states that have traditionally accepted classical liberal arguments for free enterprise,
although no pure capitalist states exist and all have forms of
mixed economies. In nations such as the United States, for instance, where rhetoric for free enterprise has been especially
strong, state intervention in economics still suffers disappro-
bation despite nearly two hundred years of increasing intervention and of strong support for intervention by the major political parties and commercial interests. Despite such negative
feeling about intervention, the Congressional Budget Office
calculates that the United States provides nearly $400 billion
annually to aid commercial activities.[6]

A critic of state intervention in the private economic sphere
admits that under certain conditions such activity is appropriate, proposing that

the question should be not whether the individual or the industry wants
a subsidy. Everyone, from the most successful businessman to the
poorest welfare recipient, "wants" something from government. The

question for society should be, instead, does the subsidy conform to the traditional standards used previously in the dispensing of federal assistance.

Does the subsidy increase competition? Does the subsidy fulfill a need that otherwise will go unfilled? Is the subsidy a legitimate part of the defense effort? Does the subsidy fulfill a humanitarian task?[7]

Other more socially oriented observers would add the question, does it promote a function that increases society's ability to function democratically? And this question has been increasingly asked as governments throughout the West have been prodded to reevaluate and expend state press aid by democratic socialists.

The increase of public policy interest in press economics has drawn criticism from those concerned about possible negative consequences, but even some of these critics see merit in certain forms of intervention. One such critic, Joseph Kaiser, has argued:

There is nothing objectionable about subsidies motivated by considerations of economic policy whose purpose is to increase productivity and assist adaptation to structural change. Newspaper companies which are given aid on the basis of these criteria are basically in the same position as companies from other sectors of the economy benefiting from similar aid, since what are decisive are the criteria of general economic policy which are applied to newspapers having regard to their position in a given complex of actual structures and functions.[8]

Despite the contributions of government intervention in press economics seen by many observers, such intervention, admittedly, can have negative effects. Obviously, there is danger of government control of expression if the government has nefarious motives or if adequate protections are not afforded against potential pressures by the government. But intervention can also damage the potential for increased diversity and public participation if it reinforces structural forms that do not promote diversity and participation, and if it does not actually aid those units of the press that most serve democratic purposes. Nevertheless, intervention has and can play an important role in serving such purposes.

CLASSES OF INTERVENTION

To explore the subject of state intervention in press economics, it is important to understand the different types of state intervention. Such intervention can be divided into three broad
classes: advantages, subsidies, and regulation. Advantages include assistance provided to the press through preferred treat-
ment or reduced fees for services by government agencies, entities, or regulated industries. These may include fiscal
advantages provided to a wide range of industries or advantages provided only to the newspaper industry. Subsidies en-
compass actual cash transfers from the government to the press.
In a less precise usage, some economists and political scientists
use the term *subsidization* interchangeably with the term *state
intervention* and the term *subsidies*, when they actually mean *advantages*. Regulation involves the efforts of government to organize and manage the structure and activities of the press.

In discussions of state intervention in press economics, however, it is necessary to use more specific terms that explain the
intent, administration, and distribution of state assistance. The
terms *direct* and *indirect* are used to indicate the manner in which
state aid is extended. Direct aid is that given directly to an individual unit of the press, while indirect aid can be described
as assistance—such as postal rate reductions—not given directly to an entity of the press but helpful to it. The terms *general* and *specific* are used to refer to aid in terms of its basic purposes. General aid is extended to assist in a newspaper's
operation, but the state does not allocate it for a specific purpose. Specific aid is provided for a specific purpose, such as acquisition or modernization of physical facilities. These terms are
sometimes used, improperly, in place of the terms *direct* and
indirect.

These four terms, however, are not descriptive enough to
cover all discussions of state involvement in media economics.
The words *interventionistic* and *noninterventionistic* are used to
describe the effects of state assistance. Interventionistic aid is
that which directly affects the economic operations of a newspaper—a cash subsidy for newsprint consumption, for instance—when the absence of such aid would immediately affect the financial situation of the newspaper. Noninterventionistic

aid has a less immediate impact on financial conditions, and includes such intervention as exemptions from paying sales taxes.

In administrative terms, aid is either *selective* or *mandated*. With selective aid, the decision to intervene directly in a particular newspaper's situation is made by an administrative body or official. With mandated aid, an administrator or official body does not have the discretion to extend or withhold aid, since the legislative mandate for the intervention stipulates what types of enterprises shall be involved and under what conditions intervention shall be made.

State intervention can also be discussed in terms of the purposes it serves; three classifications cover these purposes. First, intervention can be classified as being made to promote general conditions conducive to the health of all entities in the newspaper industry. Types of intervention that serve this purpose include exemptions from regulations with which other industries must cope, funds to help train journalists, and provision of aid and information to newspapers by government public information personnel. The second category of intervention covers activities that help the press reduce operating costs. Included in such intervention are postal rate reductions, telecommunications advantages, and exemptions from certain taxes. The third kind of intervention involves the provision of capital funds to help cover newspapers' operating expenses. This category includes subsidies, loans, and grants.

The characteristics of intervention in any nation depend greatly upon the reasons for its institution. As Anthony Smith observes:

Where the state financial intervention in the press is established on the basis of the general difficulties of the newspaper industry, subsidies tend to develop of a "general" kind. . . . When the state is considering aid on the argument that diversity of outlets is an essential prerequisite to the free flow of information, then it logically follows that the financial aid must be organized in such a way as to guarantee the desired results.[9]

TYPES OF INTERVENTION

Twelve general types of state intervention are found in Western democratic nations. They divide into the categories that will be described and illustrated on the following pages: five advantages, five subsidies, and two types of regulation.

Advantages

Taxes. Sales taxes are levied on products and services in some nations by national and subordinate government entities, but the most common form of product taxation is the national value added tax (VAT). The VAT includes incremental taxes levied on the value added to a product at each stage of its processing from raw materials to final production and, finally, distribution. Such taxes significantly increase the cost of covered products and components. Most Western nations have exempted newspaper sales from value added taxes or reduced the rate of taxation. Others have provided exemptions for or reduced taxation on the major materials needed in newspaper production, such as newsprint and ink. In some nations, distribution services for newspapers are also exempted from value added taxes.

Similarly, many subordinate entities that tax sales in order to raise revenue provide exemptions from or reductions in sales taxes. This type of intervention is indirect, mandated, and non-interventionistic. Denmark provides a zero value added tax rating for newspapers, thus sparing newspapers about 120 million Danish kroner annually,[10] an amount equivalent to about 6 percent of the aggregate annual newspaper advertising expenditures in Denmark.[11] France has set its VAT rate at 2.1 percent for the daily press, while other publications pay 4 percent.[12] Newspapers in the United States are exempted from sales taxes in the majority of states, and most do not pay sales taxes on the major products used in the manufacturing process.[13]

Many nations support the newspaper industry by providing special exemptions from taxation or avenues by which tax liabilities can be reduced. Like other businesses, newspapers in many nations can reinvest profits and reduce their pretax profits and thus their tax liability. Some nations exempt the press from some taxes altogether; and to help keep prices down, some nations provide exemptions from duties on imported newsprint. France excuses publishers from professional taxes,[14] which are based on assets and on the number of employees in a firm, while the United States exempts newspapers from excise taxes on telephone charges.[15]

Postal rates. Reductions in, and sometimes exemptions from, charges for postal delivery of newspapers are given in every Western democratic nation except Ireland. The amounts of aid vary, but all provide significant and immediate cash savings on the costs of postal delivery. This is a major advantage because many newspapers rely heavily on the postal systems for delivery outside their immediate markets. Small morning newspapers in Denmark, particularly politically oriented publications, are the heaviest users of Danish postal rate reductions—although such reductions are available to all newspapers. Taxpayers pay as much as 58 million Danish kroner for the service,[16] an amount equivalent to about 3 percent of the total Danish newspaper income from advertising. Postal rate advantages are indirect, specific, mandated, and interventionistic aid.

Telecommunication rates. Newspapers in most Western nations, particularly those whose communication industries are state owned or operated, are provided reduced service rates for telephone, telegraph, and other telecommunication services employed by the press. Like postal rate advantages, these interventions provide newspapers with important savings not enjoyed by other industries. These interventions are indirect, specific, mandated, and generally noninterventionistic—unlike postal advantages—because their absence would ordinarily not be as immediately harmful to press economics as the absence of postal advantages would be.

Italy provides a 75 percent reduction on telex, telegraph, and telephone services, and some telephone calls are free for newspapers. These advantages have an estimated value of 60 billion lire,[17] an amount equivalent to approximately 24 percent of the annual newspaper revenue from advertising.

Transportation rates. State railway systems in some nations provide reduced rates for carrying papers throughout the nation, much as postal advantages are given for similar purposes. This type of intervention is indirect, specific, mandated, and noninterventionistic. France spends approximately 35 million francs annually on this intervention,[18] an advantage equivalent to about 8 percent of newspaper advertising receipts in that nation. Some nations provide reductions for distribution of newspapers on other forms of state-operated transportation, particularly air and sea conveyances. Newspapers in Belgium, for instance, receive rate advantages on Sabena, the state-owned airline.[19]

Training and research. Funds for training and press-related research are provided in a few nations. Nearly every nation indirectly aids the press through journalism education or prejournalism education in state higher education institutions (as it does through education programs for the professions and trades). The type of advantage meant here, however, is the provision of funds to improve working journalists' knowledge and abilities and to increase information about the state of the newspaper industry. Such intervention is helpful to the industry since it allows newspaper enterprises to allocate their own funds elsewhere. This type of intervention is indirect, specific, selective, and noninterventionistic. It is found in the United States, for example, where tax dollars support advanced training for journalists through special education and training programs of the National Endowment for the Humanities.[20]

Subsidies

Grants/operation subsidies. This category encompasses a variety of aid programs in which cash is provided to newspapers to help pay the costs of newspaper production and distribution, to encourage practices that will make papers operate more efficiently, or to fill social needs—such as newspapers in secondary languages—that would not be met by the commercial marketplace. In France, for instance, the state helps some papers survive by providing funds to papers that receive little advertising because of their ideological or theological leanings.[21] In the past, the communist paper *L'Humanite*, the Catholic paper *La Croix*, and the papers *La Quotidien de Paris* and *Liberation* have been funded.

The Swedish government provides direct production subsidies to papers competing against another paper that dominates a given market. The amounts provided are based on the amount of newsprint devoted to editorial content. The government provides other funds to start new papers and help existing papers expand their markets.[22] In the Netherlands, papers receive cash payments from the government to compensate them for revenues lost after the introduction of advertising on state television.[23] Newspapers in Austria that are distributed in more than one province receive grants from the state to help cover the additional costs of their broader activities.[24]

Joint distribution subsidies are extended in some nations to encourage newspapers to enter into cooperative distribution programs and thus reduce operating costs. Governments provide rebates on each copy distributed as incentives for papers to join these programs. These papers also enjoy lessened operating costs because they may reduce their circulation staffs and operations. All but one daily newspaper in Sweden now participate in the joint distribution program operating there.[25]

Joint distribution has been one of the most widely accepted interventions in Norway and Sweden because it helps remove the labor-intensive aspect of distribution for each paper and introduces cost-effective and income-generating systems. These systems also make it unnecessary to set up separate private distribution systems in order to enter new markets. This permits the circulation of papers in areas that might not be profitably distributed if the papers had to establish and maintain their own separate distribution systems. The result of these joint operations is the availability of a wider variety of papers throughout the countries, thus reducing the monopolization of markets due to newspaper mortality.

Newspapers entering joint production agreements whereby they use the same printing facilities receive special subsidies in Norway and Sweden. This aid is given to help establish modern printing facilities that can be cooperatively operated in a cost-effective manner, thus replacing duplicate, outdated, and inefficiently run production facilities.[26] Such assistance is also given to promote joint purchasing organizations and schemes for cooperative advertising practices and production. Despite the obvious cost benefits of such cooperation, very few companies have taken advantage of the available subsidies. Why the stimulus to reduce costs and improve facilities and services through cooperative subsidies has not been effective is unclear.

This type of intervention is direct, specific, mandated, and interventionistic, but it is available for only a limited period, during which the joint venture is planned and initiated. Because they are direct and interventionistic, the subsidies discussed in this section have caused much concern among libertarians. Most of this aid appears to be general in character and can be either selective or mandated, although mandated programs seem most prevalent.

Loans. Loan programs have been instituted in some nations to provide funds for newspapers at reduced rates. The funds are used for modernizing equipment and facilities so that newspapers can compete more economically. In most cases, these loans have been made available to firms that could not receive credit in the commercial credit market because of their economic conditions, or to firms that could not receive funds on terms as economically advantageous as those that large companies are able to negotiate. These loans are direct, specific, and interventionistic. In most cases, the decision to extend a loan is made selectively, according to general guidelines laid down in the creation of the loan fund.

Depending on their location, the loan funds can be operated either directly by governments or through nongovernmental funding organizations to which the government contributes, or for which the government guarantees credit. In Sweden, the government operates the loan fund,[27] but Denmark has opted for a state-supported foundation to reduce government involvement in the decision-making process.[28]

Government advertising. Governments provide considerable income for many newspapers through advertisements for state-run companies, government agencies, and decision-making bodies. While government advertising expenditures are important to newspapers, they generally have not been formulated as public aid programs. Rather, they serve the informational and commercial aspects of the state. In some countries specific rules guide the placement of such advertising, requiring the government to spread the advertising around to competing papers. In Norway, for instance, government departments wishing to place national ads must put them in all of the nation's newspapers. The annual government advertising budget for Norway amounts to about 60 million Norwegian kroner,[29] about 3 percent of total newspaper advertising receipts. Advertising is a direct, specific, and generally noninterventionistic type of assistance and is employed in most advanced Western democratic nations.

News agency aid. Because they realize the importance of news flow, some countries help national news agencies cover the costs of distribution by telegraph and by radio. These aid programs are similar to grants and operating subsidies provided directly to newspapers. From the standpoint of newspapers, this type of intervention is indirect, specific, and noninterventionistic. From the standpoint of the news agencies, it is direct, usually general, mandated, and often interventionistic.

Party aid. Party aid is provided in some Scandinavian nations to promote the informational activities of the political organizations. Some of this aid reaches sympathetic newspapers when the parties act as conduits for the funds. Since 1965, the Swedish government has distributed 23 million kroner annually to the parties, according to their representation in the parliament.[30]

Regulation

Ownership regulation. This type of intervention includes the regulation of newspaper ownership by individuals and corporations. It also includes regulation of the number of papers that may be owned and of the markets in which they may be owned. Though ownership regulation varies, it generally involves anti-cartel laws. In some nations special press ownership laws restrict foreign ownership.

Newspaper ownership in Germany, for instance, comes under the surveillance of the anti-cartel agency. Any merger that would make the joint turnover of the new company exceed 25 million deutsche marks must receive the permission of the Bundeskartellamt, the federal cartel agency.[31] Anti-cartel regulations also require the reporting of smaller newspaper mergers. The ownership regulations in Germany have been ineffectual in halting mergers, since the cartel agency has felt compelled to permit mergers that create monopolies when the alternative is death for one of the papers.

Price regulation. Some nations intervene in press economics by regulating circulation prices and prices of essential production products. The Comitato Prezzi del Ministero dell'Industria fixes the prices of newspapers and such products as newsprint as part of its responsibilities for keeping down the costs of politically sensitive Italian goods.[32] Price regulation in the newspaper industry was not instituted as part of a program to attain a specific economic goal within the newspaper industry. Rather, it is part of the general control of prices within Italian society. Although the regulation keeps circulation prices low and prevents fluctuation in the prices of newspaper supplies, its main purpose is general price stability as part of the nation's macroeconomic policies. In most nations with price controls, such regulation in the newspaper industry appears to be similarly motivated.

DANGERS OF INTERVENTION

That early suggestions for new intervention raised concern about possible negative consequences in not surprising. State intervention often played a role in journalistic enterprises during the early days of printing, but it came to be regarded as bribery and was generally rejected as democratic rule developed and newspapers began asserting independence from government. Many warnings about accepting favors have become platitudes in modern society. Martial (c. 40-c.104 A.D.), for instance, warned, "Gifts are like fishhooks: for who is not aware that the greedy char is deceived by the fly he swallows?"[33] More recently, Otto von Bismarck (1815–1898) reminded, "He who has his thumb on the purse has the power."[34]

As increased intervention in press economics began receiving consideration in the decades following the Second World War, similar warnings were sounded. In 1961 a Young Fabian publication in the United Kingdom warned, "No one who believes in freedom can accept the principle of a State subsidy to the press."[35] Later, Cecil King of the International Publishing Corporation told a meeting of the Institute of Journalists, "So far as I am aware, journalistic ingenuity has not found a way of tapping government money on any large scale which would be acceptable to government and public opinion, which could be distributed fairly and which would not threaten the independence of papers."[36]

When Ralph Lowenstein created the Press Independence and Critical Ability Index in the mid-1960s, he dismissed all government loans to the press, direct subsidies, differential tax rates on the press, and dependency on government advertising as negative factors and automatically calculated them as threats to press freedom.[37] This reflected the current attitude toward state intervention, an attitude based upon observation of the use of subsidies in nondemocratic nations in the Second and Third worlds and upon similar use of subsidies to influence press content during the development of Western democratic states.

In his consideration of the increasing support for intervention, Antero Pietila in 1969 noted the insufficiency of the existing arguments against support in democratic nations:

Subsidies to the press to date have often been used not necessarily as a measure to bolster the press but rather to ensure its acquiescence and cooperation for purposes deemed advantageous by the advocate of the bill, in most cases by the government . . . little if anything is known about the effects of a government subsidy system on freedom of the press in a democratically ruled nation.[38]

As intervention increased in the following years, the shallow, knee-jerk reactions to assistance and concerns about potential harmful effects decreased to the point where the Royal Commission on the Press (United Kingdom) reported, "It would perhaps not be unduly cynical to suggest that steadfast defences of editorial freedom have tended to grow less enthusiastic as the economic position of the press has declined further."[39]

Most of the early and the emerging, more sophisticated criticism of state intervention revolved around two potential dangers: 1) that government control of the administration of advantages and subsidies would help political allies in the newspaper industry, and 2) that newspaper dependence on funds for survival would lead to government coercion of publishers into supporting, or at least not opposing, government desires. Much of the criticism focused on suggestions for direct assistance through subsidies. In response, methods for protecting against the two potential dangers emerged. An FIEJ (Federation Internationale des Editors de Journaux et Publications) resolution of 1976, endorsed by the International Press Institute, argued, "Measures of government assistance, in countries which have such, must exclude any possibility of government pressure on the recipient and must be established by law."[40] Although the federation supported protective measures, it did not suggest a model statute, leaving it up to each nation to construct laws appropriate for its situation.

Critics of intervention argued most strongly against selective support and urged automatic rules for extension of aid, rules that would prevent official discretion in the awarding of assistance. The apparent support for a few selective support programs brought the following suggestions from an observer who was worried about the possible effects of state intervention:

Selective support for the press, used judiciously and fairly, may indeed be necessary to prevent papers from dying out. But no other criteria should apply than the financial situation of the papers and their position among competitors. Under no circumstances must selective support be employed to influence the structure of the press according to the inclination of any government or parliament in power at a particular time.[41]

Francisco Labrado noted the dangers of selective aids, but suggested that these aids could be extended without endangering press freedom if specific criteria guided decisions about aid distribution.

Obviously the use of priority criteria introduces a difficult problem to be solved at a practical level and risks of pressures and discrimination by the powers. Because of this [risk] there will always be necessary an objective definition of the norms and criteria for the aid allotment whose definition ought to be public, worked out with the participation of representatives from the profession and from society, and controlled by the organization the representatives come from.[42]

As a result of the concerns raised during the period in which intervention began increasing (1965–1970), most nations first attempted to increase advantages rather than subsidies because advantages are generally perceived to pose less danger. In the past decade and a half, however, many nations have turned to subsidization when advantages have not stemmed the tide of newspaper mortality and concentration of ownership. Because of the fear of selective support, most of these nations have organized their support so as to guard against the dangers of intervention. They have done this mostly by instituting protective administrative structures and procedures.

Nations engaging in direct intervention have generally selected three basic protective policies to guide the administration of subsidies: 1) distribution of aid according to fixed guidelines, whenever possible; 2) organization of administrative bodies that must make selective decisions along nonpartisan lines, bodies that include representatives of the public and professional organizations; and 3) operation of the aid process in an open manner, to preclude charges of favoritism behind closed doors. But attempts to protect the integrity of intervention have caused additional problems since nonselective support through advantages, subsidization, and regulation can be counterproductive by assisting all papers rather than only those that need it most. Freiberg has pointed out the nature of this additional danger: "The smaller, independent enterprises need these extra funds to survive, while the larger corporate press groups use the funds to expand their domination through further takeovers."[43]

Labrado has also indicated that this can be a serious problem. Aid criteria generally mandate larger amounts of aid for the larger units of the press, and decisions to extend aid are based on such factors as circulation, income, and newsprint consumption. These criteria backfire, he says, " . . . because the newspapers receiving more aid are those with greater circulation, greater advertising income and greater number of pages. The opinion press, on the other hand, ends up relatively unprotected as a result of its low circulation and low advertising income."[44]

The broad rules for assistance have also resulted in aid going to all units of the press, regardless of their content. This has led the International Federation of Journalists to recommend recently that "assistance should normally be granted only to newspapers and other periodicals published with an eye to the general interest for the purposes of public instruction, education and information." This would halt the flow of public funds to the "escapist press . . . heart throb press and sensationalist press," according to the federation.[45]

A related danger of state intervention comes from what G. William Domhoff has called the "special-interest process." This process consists of what he calls "the several means by which individuals, families, corporations and business sectors within the ruling class obtain tax breaks, favors, subsidies and procedural rulings that are beneficial to their short-run interests."[46] Joel Lewels, Jr. indicates that this process was involved in the awarding of antitrust relief in the United States through the Newspaper Preservation Act.

> In its haste to pass the bill, many Congressmen showed little ability to see beyond their own special interests to the effects that the law would have on the basic issue of press freedom. They failed to prove satisfactorily to the public that the joint operations have anything to do with failing newspapers or that they are anything more than monopolistic arrangements for dividing markets and profits. Adding to this is substantial evidence indicating that the affected newspapers used every power at their command, including what amounts to bribery, to steamroll the bill into law.[47]

Another danger of subsidies and advantages is that once they are enacted and accepted by members of the industry for whom they are intended, it becomes difficult for the state to end the program, even if the need for the assistance passes. One observer has noted: "Experience teaches that subsidy programs, once established, long outlast the emergency or other need that was the occasion for their adoption. Vested interests quickly develop and strenuously fight proposals that would adversely affect them."[48]

Despite the dangers of state intervention, the state has steadily entered the realm of press economics in recent decades, but only occasional criticisms of conduct have arisen. Most of these have involved the fact that the intervention is *too fair* (i.e., it does not discriminate appropriately in the provisions of advantages, subsidies, and regulation) or that the intervention, while overtly helping all units of the press, was instituted to aid a particular unit or group of units.

The impact of intervention on the vehicles for diversity of opinion and on the avenues of public expression has not been as strong as might be anticipated, given the rhetoric behind the intervention of the past two decades. Intervention appears to have been moderately successful in slowing newspaper mortality where significant production subsidies and their programs for providing cash to newspapers have been instituted, but there has been little increase in opportunity for citizen expression. Few new papers have emerged to replace those that have died.

The bulk of state intervention in press economics is in the form that has developed during the 300-year history of the press in the Western world, intervention not designed to promote diversity. Only the intervention since the 1960s seems directly intended to preserve and extend diversity by providing a form of welfare for those units of the press that could not otherwise survive. Ownership regulation has increased and has apparently slowed concentration of ownership into the largest firms—such as those of Axel Springer and Robert Hersant—but ownership of small- and medium-sized papers has become more concentrated.

There is clearly a conflict between some of the new selective interventions and many of the interventions that have been undertaken on behalf of all newspapers but do nothing to support the goals of diversity and unit plurality. Despite such problems, many journalists and political figures support intervention, and there is little opposition. The potential for abuse is not yet viewed as severe. Colin Legum and John Cornwell have discussed the problem in a report for the Twentieth Century Fund.

Any media organization funded by government runs the risks of domination and interference, and while the danger must be faced and discussed, it should be viewed in perspective. . . . The extent to which government sponsorship constitutes a danger to the freedom, truth and accuracy of the media clearly depends on the number of checks and balances in a given situation. Should one automatically dismiss Agence France Presse and the BBC as suspect on the ground that they are both government sponsored?[49]

Scandinavian intervention has drawn the most interest from observers because many direct subsidies and selective support measures are offered. Yet evidence of abuse has yet to develop. John Merrill and Harold Fisher have noted this to be the case with Swedish intervention. Based on their interviews with a variety of Swedish publishers and journalists, they say, "Although there is theoretical danger these government-supported grants could lead to curtailment of press freedom, to date government interference has not even been hinted."[50]

Einar Ostgaard, based on his observations, interviews, and review of intervention in other Scandinavian countries as well, has reported: "There is very little danger, if any, that the measure will restrict the freedom of the press to write what it likes, to criticize government or anyone else. I think that also the danger of measures being used to favor blatantly any paper or group of papers, at least over time, is very small and in practice negligible."[51] Leonard Sussman, director of the politically conservative Freedom House, is also not hostile to state intervention: "As in so many things in life, you have to choose among evils. . . . A subsidy may not be the best way. But, if without it, the free press goes out of business, then it may be necessary."[52]

INTERVENTION BY NATION

The types and amounts of intervention vary from nation to nation, but it has been possible to gain some comparative insight into the intervention of Western nations. A list of types of assistance offered in each country has been compiled (Table 5.1). From that compilation, each type of intervention has been ranked according to the number of nations adopting it (Table 5.2), and nations have been ranked according to the total number of types of intervention in each (Table 5.3).

The most common interventions, found in all Western countries, are tax advantages and government advertising expenditures. Postal rate advantages are found in about 90 percent of the countries, and funds for educational endeavors for journalists or for journalism research are provided in three-quarters of the nations. Telecommunication rate advantages and direct

Table 5.1
Types and Number of Intervention by Nation, Frequencies of Intervention by Nation, and Intervention Time

	Tax Rates	Postal Rates	Tele. Rates	Trans. Rates	Educ./Research	Grants/Subsidies	Loans	Gov't Ads	Agency Aid	Party Aid	Owner. Reg.	Price Reg.	No. of Types	Percentages
Austria	X	X	X	X		X		X					6	50
Belgium	X	X	X	X	X	X		X				X	8	66
Canada	X	X			X	X		X			X		6	50
Denmark	X	X			X		X	X					5	42
Finland	X	X	X	X	X	X		X	X	X			9	75
France	X	X	X	X	X	X		X	X		X	X	10	83
Germany	X	X	X		X		X	X			X		7	58
Iceland	X						X	X		X		X	5	42
Ireland	X				X	X		X					4	33
Italy	X	X	X	X		X	X	X	X		X	X	10	83
Netherlands	X	X	X	X	X	X	X	X			X	X	10	83
Norway	X	X	X	X	X	X	X	X	X	X			10	83
Sweden	X	X	X	X	X	X	X	X	X	X	X		11	92
Switzerland	X	X	X		X			X					5	42
United Kingdom	X	X						X			X	X	5	42
United States	X	X			X			X			X		5	42
Frequency of Intervention	16	14	10	8	12	10	7	16	5	4	8	6	–	–
Percentages	100	87.5	62.5	50	75	62.5	43.8	100	31.3	25	50	37.5	–	–

grants and subsidies are found in nearly two-thirds of Western nations, and transportation rate advantages and ownership regulations are found in half of the countries. The remaining types of intervention are found in less than half of the nations, with subsidies for political parties being the least common. Only four types of intervention—party aid, news agency aid, price

Table 5.2
Ranking of Intervention by Nations Adopting

		Number of Nations	Percent of Total
1	Tax rate advantages	16	100
	Government advertising	16	100
3	Postal rate advantages	14	87.5
4	Education/research grants	12	75
5	Telecommunication rate advantages	10	62.5
	Grants/Subsidies	10	62.5
7	Transportation rate advantages	8	50
	Ownership regulation	8	50
9	Loans	7	43.8
10	Price regulation	6	37.5
11	News agency aid	5	31.3
12	Party Aid	4	25

regulation, and loans—are unavailable in more than half of the nations in Western Europe and North America. Sweden tops the list for total number of types of intervention, with 11 out of a possible 12. Italy, France, the Netherlands, and Norway are tied for second, with ten types of intervention each. A plurality of nations have at least half of the types of intervention. The nation with the fewest types of state intervention is Ireland, with four.

In another study, I conducted a system of assigning weighting numbers, based on the extent to which a particular type of intervention limits or alters competitive situations or the existing structures of the newspaper industry, in order to allow a rough comparison of the intensity of types of intervention and the cumulative significance of the intervention.[53] Weighted scores for intervention in each nation were calculated and the nations ranked according to the amount of intervention. In that rank-

Table 5.3
Ranking of Nations by Number of Types of Intervention

Position	Nation	Number of Types
1	Sweden	11
2	France	10
	Italy	10
	Netherlands	10
	Norway	10
6	Finland	9
7	Belgium	8
8	Germany	7
9	Austria	6
	Canada	6
11	Denmark	5
	United States of America	5
	Iceland	5
	Switzerland	5
	United Kingdom	5
16	Ireland	4

ing, Sweden again occupied the top position. Italy and the Netherlands were second, and France and Norway were in the fourth and fifth positions. The nation with the lowest combined intervention intensity was Switzerland (Table 5.4). When the nations were divided into three categories of intervention based on the total intervention scores, no nation fell into the slight intervention category, but several fell into the moderate intervention group. Not surprisingly, three Scandinavian nations were in the heavy intervention category, along with Italy, France, and the Netherlands.

In general, these indicators of the kinds of intervention adopted and the intensity of intervention bear out the contention that intervention and socialist public policy are related. The

Table 5.4
Ranking of Nations by Weighted Score for Total Intervention

Ranking	Nation	Weighted Score	
1	Sweden	19.2	
2	Italy	17.8	
	Netherlands	17.8	Heavy Intervention
4	France	17.6	
5	Norway	16.6	
6	Finland	14.8	
7	Belgium	13.4	
8	Germany	11.4	
9	Canada	11.0	
10	Austria	10.8	
11	Iceland	10.2	Moderate Intervention
12	United Kingdom	9.6	
13	United States	8.6	
14	Denmark	7.8	
15	Ireland	7.4	
16	Switzerland	7.0	

nations with the most intervention are also the nations with the most intense intervention; traditionally they have strong socialist parties or mixed economies. The nations that intervene less tend to have stronger capitalistic tendencies, or mixed economies with strong nonsocialist parties.

PRESS INTERVENTION POLICIES AND NATIONAL ECONOMIC POLICY

Another exploration of state intervention found four major patterns of intervention among Western nations. It determined that these patterns roughly correspond to the general macro-

Table 5.5
Grouping of Nations by Intervention Pattern

```
Group 1:  The Capitalism Augmentor

          Austria
          Ireland
          Belgium
          Finland

Group 2:  The Capitalism Restrictor

          Italy
          The Netherlands
          United Kingdom
          France

Group 3:  The Capitalism Supervisor

          Germany
          Denmark
          United States
          Switzerland

Group 4:  The Welfare Capitalist

          Sweden
          Canada
          Norway

Not Grouped

          Iceland
```

economic policies of groups of nations (Table 5.5). A fifth pattern, which included only Iceland, was discovered merely because it is different from the other patterns. Because this pattern includes only one nation, it is not included in this discussion as a major pattern of intervention.[54]

The first pattern includes Austria, Belgium, Finland, and Ireland, and has a private enterprise orientation. The group generally eschews regulation and subsidization of the press, but supports newspapers through fiscal advantages. Nations in this group provide some grants and subsidies to media, but generally limit such intervention to programs intended to augment the efforts of private, profit-oriented newspapers. Subsidy programs aimed at increasing the availability of newspapers in areas where they would not normally be circulated, and programs aimed at ensuring the availability of material in secondary languages are examples of the subsidies this group provides. Because its pattern of intervention is predominantly one of supporting and augmenting capitalistic competition, this group was named the Capitalism Augmentor.

The second pattern is seen in a group of nations whose press policies have a state capitalism orientation. Nations in this group include France, Italy, the Netherlands, and the United Kingdom. They engage in policies intended to restrict capitalistic competition in the newspaper industry and to limit the effects of existing competition. The group was called the Capitalism Restrictor. This group also provides financial assistance through advantages and subsidies to ensure the continued existence of newspapers that would probably not otherwise be able to survive in an economically competitive marektplace. This group uses price regulation and ownership regulation to control competition.

Denmark, Germany, Switzerland, and the United States constitute the third group of nations, called the Capitalism Supervisor. This group is made up of the strongest supporters of private enterprise in the West, and it intervenes in press economics mainly through fiscal advantages. Direct press subsidies are generally not provided, although some members of the group provide subsidies through loan programs. Despite its private enterprise orientation, the group regulates press ownership—however cursorily—through antitrust mechanisms. This group's regulation of activities however, is not as strong as that of the second group, the Capitalism Restrictor.

The final group pursues economic policies intended to reduce the damaging effects of a competitive marketplace by providing state assistance to those whom capitalistic competition harms or disadvantages; it was named the Welfare Capitalist group. Despite the interventionist orientation, this group does not attempt to restrict competition to the extent that the second group does. Nations included in this group are Norway, Sweden, and Canada.

Just as all nations in this study intervene in press economics to some degree, all Western nations intervene in economics generally. The days of *laissez-faire* capitalism are long past, if indeed they ever existed. All the nations in this study engage in state economic planning and pursue some form of simple or state monopoly capitalism. Most of the nations engage in state monopoly capitalism, a form of economic activity in which the state overrides the freedom of the marketplace through a variety of tax, public ownership, and monetary policies. The remaining nations engage in forms of simple monopoly capitalism, which breaks from *laissez-faire* capitalism and permits the state to engage in relatively low levels of economic planning and activity to promote general conditions for a healthy economy and to maintain order in the marketplace for goods.

Most of the nations in this study (the most notable exception being the United States) are clearly welfare states, i.e., nations with comprehensive social welfare systems that extend basic social services to all members of society. Some nations that provide the most extensive welfare programs to ameliorate inequities caused by capitalism continue to maintain class divisions while carrying out significant state planning or public ownership policies, or subsidizing industry and maintaining and promoting competition. They are known as welfare capitalist states.

The nations of the first group in terms of press policy—Austria, Belgium, Ireland, and Finland—pursue macroeconomic policies that include relatively moderate levels of state monopoly capitalism and provide a range of social welfare programs. The group's pattern of press intervention is thus consistent with the general economic policies of moderate intervention.

Nations in the second group—Italy, France, the Netherlands, and the United Kingdom—most strongly regulate the press and are predominantly state monopoly capitalist states, with strong central governments that engage in extensive economic planning, public ownership, and social welfare programs. The group's press intervention pattern is thus generally consistent with the macroeconomic policies that show a distrust of capitalism.

The third group—Denmark, Germany, Switzerland, and the United States—is made up of nations most closely allied with simple monopoly capitalism. These nations have federal systems that disperse government power through lower levels of government, thus reducing the ability to effectively engage in central economic planning and control even if the nations should desire to engage in more significant economic intervention. As a result, economic intervention is generally at a lower level than would be expected of nations far more distrustful of capitalism, or those with central governments. This group's pattern of press intervention is thus generally consistent with its economic intervention as a whole.

Nations in the fourth group—Canada, Sweden, and Norway—significantly subsidize the press and also pursue the strongest general welfare capitalist economic policies of the nations in this study. As state monopoly capitalist nations, these countries engage in significant intervention for the purpose of organizing economic activity and aiding individuals and companies disadvantaged by the competitive economic system.

Of the four groups, group 2 and group 4 include the nations with the most types of intervention and the interventions with the highest intensity levels. In terms of press intervention policy, these nations were located in the heavy intervention category. If these two groups of nations are considered in terms of general macroeconomic policy, one would expect them also to have the highest levels of government consumption expenditures in terms of the Gross Domestic Product (GDP). This is in fact the case. The mean percentage of GDP consumed by these states—a standard indicator of government economic activity—is 19 (Table 5.6).

The moderate levels of press intervention practiced by groups 1 and 3 would lead one to predict a lower level of government involvement in the GDP than that of groups 2 and 4. This is also shown to be the case. The mean percentage of government consumption expenditures of the Gross Domestic Product for nations in groups 1 and 3 is 18—and this figure is skewed upward because military spending in such nations as the United States, the United Kingdom, and Germany is double that of most European nations. The four patterns of intervention represented by the groups of nations provide explanations of press intervention behavior and provide a view of press intervention policy that is thus consistent with the nations' general macroeconomic policies.

Table 5.6
Percentage of Gross Domestic Product (GDP) Consumed by Government Expenditures, Listed by Factor

Factor	Percentage
Factor I	
Austria	18
Belgium	17
Finland	19
Ireland	19
Mean for Factor I	18
Factor II	
France	15
Italy	14
Netherlands	18
United Kingdom	20
Mean for Factor II	19
Factor III	
Denmark	24
Germany	20
Switzerland	13
United States of America	18
Mean for Factor III	19
Factor IV	
Canada	20
Norway	18
Sweden	29
Mean for Factor IV	22
Factor V	
Iceland	12
Mean for Factor V	12

Source: "Expenditures of GDP," 1979/80 *Statistical Yearbook* (New York: United Nations, Department of International Economic and Social Affairs, 1981), pp. 648–662.

Nations in the Capitalism Augmentor and Capitalism Supervisor groups intervene at low levels and support the commercial marketplace of ideas. But the Capitalism Augmentor group—whose nations have been more responsive to the influences of democratic socialist and socialist ideology than those in the Capitalism Supervisor group—steps in to supplement the economic marketplace.

Nations in the Capitalism Restrictor and Welfare Capitalism groups intervene more strongly in press economics and show two distinct approaches to intervention. The Welfare Capitalism group is made up of states strongly influenced by democratic socialist ideology. It provides significant subsidies and advantages—especially to units of the press that are disadvantaged by competition—while at the same time supporting competition. This policy is seen in the group's rejection of price regulations. The Capitalism Restrictor group, however, restricts competition. Although it provides stronger subsidization and advantages than do the nations of the two market-oriented factors, groups 1 and 3, it relies on regulation rather than subsidies to combat the problems caused by a commercial marketplace for ideas. That the nations of this factor should pursue such anti-competitive policies is not surprising when one considers that socialist and communist parties have played major roles in developing the economic policies of these states.

FOUR PROPOSITIONS

A review of the history of state intervention in newspaper finances during the past three centuries and its modern practice leads me to propose the following.

1. The character of state intervention in press economics depends upon the nature of the relationship between the state and its citizens. When citizens are subservient to the state, as was the case of most Western nations in the seventeenth and eighteenth centuries, intervention will be authoritarian or seductive and will be used to gain the press's acquiescence. As states become more democratic and individual liberty increases, the intervention becomes less coercive.

2. State intervention expands and contracts in accordance to the economic needs of the press. The amount of intervention is determined by the press's financial stability. Intervention will increase to meet the press's minimum financial requirements and will decrease when these requirements are satisfied by outside sources.

3. The types of state intervention are shaped by the political-economic tenets accepted in a particular nation. The dominant political and economic philosophies, or their accepted interpretations, will determine the nature and forms of intervention in a given state, regardless of the forms of intervention selected by other states at comparable levels of economic and democratic development.

4. In any given nation, state intervention in press economics will parallel intervention in the economy as a whole. State press policies will be consistent with economic policies pursued in other industries and in the general economy.

INFLUENCES ON INTERVENTION

A previous analysis of state intervention sought to establish the relationship between several of these economic, demographic, political, and media use variables, and the levels of state intervention.[55] The study was undertaken to determine what influence, if any, these factors had on the amounts of intervention in a particular nation. Thus the study allowed predictions about the effects of the variables on intervention levels. Such a predictive capacity is useful in public policy discussions and decision making, and it affords a clearer view of the factors that relate to state intervention.

The possible influences on intervention tested in the study were percentage of newspaper mortality since the Second World War, percentage of total advertising expenditures spent for newspaper advertising, the existence of television competition for advertising, newspaper circulation per 1,000 people, per capita consumption of newsprint (in pounds), size of nation (in square miles), population, number of languages in the country, number of political parties, political orientation, press tradition (political or commercial), and the presence and effectiveness of a press council.[56] The best single predictor of intervention was found to be press tradition. High levels of intervention can be predicted from a political press tradition, and low levels of intervention can be predicted from a commercial press tradition. Under the political press tradition, the press is structured and operated to support a particular political party or viewpoint, or is associated with or owned by a political party. The term *polit-*

ical press tradition also refers to situations in which previous political affiliations continue to dominate the structure and operation of the press. Under the commercial press tradition, the
press is operated chiefly to generate profit, rather than to carry
political views and debate.

The study used three factors to determine whether poor economic conditions for newspapers are an important impetus for
higher intervention. Newspaper mortality, the most commonly
cited reason for increasing intervention in many Western states,
was discovered *not* to be a significant predictor of intervention.
The same was true for the percentage of advertising expenditures going to newspaper advertising. Only the presence of TV
advertising was a significant predictor of intervention, and it
affected intervention differently than one might anticipate. Although it was expected that the presence of TV advertising
would correlate with higher intervention (because it was assumed that television ads would attract revenue previously
available to newspapers, and thus harm the economic condition of newspapers), the *absence* of television advertising corre-
lated with intervention. The three factors, then, do not support
the argument that poor economic conditions lead to high state
intervention in press economics. The study also addressed the
question of whether low newspaper use among the public leads
to higher intervention. It found that while readership is relatively high among states with high intervention, the amount of
newsprint consumed is low—an indication that the amount of
editorial and advertising information made available in the
newspapers is limited. The study did not support the argument that low newspaper use leads to intervention, although
there was evidence that the quantity of material (and presumably the use in terms of the amount of time that readers devoted to papers) was low.

The third issue addressed in the study was whether the
amount of political diversity in a nation is related to intervention. It was believed that high levels of political diversity—indicated by the number of political parties and the press tradition of the country—would lead to high intervention. The study
found that as the number of political parties increases, the
amount of intervention increases. This is presumably the case

because of the belief that the state should provide funds to ensure the survival of diverse media, so that viewpoints of various parties can be conveyed. This belief is the basis of the democratic socialist press in the West today. Press tradition, as indicated earlier, was also a significant factor: nations with a political, rather than commercial, press tradition engaged in higher levels of intervention.

The finding that the highest levels of state intervention cannot be attributed to national political orientation to the left side of the political spectrum does not contradict the argument that democratic socialist philosophy has had a significant impact on Western press policies. Two of the six nations with the highest levels of intervention, France and the Netherlands, have had traditional political orientations dominated, respectively, by center-conservative and center political parties. At the same time, the two countries have had significant socialist parties within their political systems.

Because high newspaper mortality has not occurred in those nations with the highest levels of state intervention in press economics—Sweden, Italy, and Norway, for example—the intervention cannot be directly attributed to high levels of newspaper mortality. However, fears that the high levels of mortality found in certain nations might occur in countries with great political diversity may well have induced increased intervention in press economics before the situation deteriorated, and the intervention may have slowed mortality. High levels of state intervention in press economics in democratic states cannot be attributed merely to efforts to save a commercially inviable press. They are better attributed to the desire to promote and preserve the possibility for diverse viewpoints to be made available in the marketplace of ideas, a basic requirement under the democratic socialist approach to the press.

NOTES

1. Simopekka Nortamo, "Helsingin Sanomat Editor Warns That Selective Forms of Government Subsidies to Newspapers Constitute Real Threat to Freedom of the Press," *IPI Report* 26 (January 1977): 11.

2. James O'Connor, "The Fiscal Crisis of the State," in Robert B.

Carson, Jerry Ingles, and Douglas McLaud, eds., *Government in the American Economy* (Lexington, Mass.: D.C. Heath, 1973), 188–207.

3. J. W. Freiberg, *The French Press: Class, State, and Ideology* (New York: Praeger, 1981), 12–13.

4. Ibid., 166.

5. Anthony Smith, "State Intervention and the Management of the Press," in James Curran, ed., *The British Press: A Manifesto* (London: Macmillan Press, 1978), 53–72.

6. Congressional Budget Office, "Federal Support of U.S. Business" (Washington, D.C.: U.S. Government Printing Office, 1984).

7. Leonard Baker, *The Guaranteed Society* (New York: Macmillan, 1968), 218.

8. Joseph H. Kaiser, *Press Planning: The State and Newspaper Publishing in Germany* (Zurich: International Press Institute, 1975), 68.

9. Smith, 1978, 64.

10. Aage Erhardtsen, *Evolution of Concentration and Competition in the Danish Newspaper and Magazine Sector*, Evolution of Concentration and Competition Series, no. 10 (Brussels: Commission of the European Communities, 1978), 25.

11. Standard international statistical sources do not report data on the gross product of newspapers separately, so data cannot be used as a baseline to judge the significance of the amounts of money the national newspaper industries save through various subventions. The most readily available statistic is the expenditures for newspaper advertising. In most Western nations advertising accounts for 60–70 percent of newspaper revenues.

12. Anthony Smith, "Subsidies and the Press in Europe," *Political and Economic Planning* 43 (1977): 13.

13. "The Struggle Goes On over State Taxes," *Presstime* 3 (December 1981): 16.

14. George Thomas Kurian, ed., *World Press Encyclopedia* (New York: Facts on File, 1982), 1: 354.

15. Herbert Lee Williams, *Newspaper Organization and Management*, 5th ed. (Ames, Iowa: Iowa State University Press, 1978), 374.

16. Erhardtsen, 25.

17. Smith, 1977, 32.

18. Ibid., 14.

19. Ibid., 77.

20. See National Endowment for the Humanities, *Sixteenth Annual Report 1981* (Washington, D. C.: U.S. Government Printing Office, 1982).

21. Smith, 1977, 14–15.

22. Karl Erik Gustafsson and Stig Hadenius, *Swedish Press Policy* (Stockholm: The Swedish Institute, 1976), 76–100.

23. Maria Brouwer, *A Study of the Evolution of Concentration in the Dutch Press, Magazines and Schoolbooks Publishing Industries*, Evolution of Concentration and Competition Series, no. 16 (Brussels: Commission of the European Communities, 1978), 48.

24. Smith, 1977, 91.

25. Gustafsson and Hadenius, 92–94.

26. Milton Hollstein, "Are Newspaper Subsidies Unthinkable?" *Columbia Journalism Review* 17 (May/June 1978): 16.

27. Olof Hulten, *Mass Media and State Support in Sweden* (Stockholm: The Swedish Institute, 1979), 13.

28. Erhardtsen, 31–33.

29. Smith, 1977, 52.

30. Robert Picard, "State Aid and the Press: A Case Study of Newspapers in Two Swedish Cities, 1965–1978" (M.A. thesis, California State University, Fullerton, 1979), 70.

31. Smith, 1977, 22–23.

32. Ibid., 28–29.

33. Martial, *Epigrams*, Book VI, 63, 5.

34. Speech to the North German Reichstag, March 11, 1867. Quoted in John Bartlett, *Familiar Quotations*, 4th ed. (Boston: Little, Brown and Co., 1968), 677.

35. Peter Benensen, *A Free Press*, Fabian Research Series, no. 223 (London: The Fabian Society, 1961), 22.

36. "Subsidies and Press Freedom," *IPI Report* 15 (March 1967): 6.

37. Ralph Lowenstein, "Measuring World Press Freedom as a Political Indicator" (Ph.D. diss., University of Missouri-Columbia, 1967).

38. Antero Pietila, "Government Subsidies and Press Freedom: The Case of Sweden" (M.A. thesis, Southern Illinois University, 1969), 69.

39. Royal Commission on the Press, "Press Subsidies in Foreign Countries," unpublished report, 1976.

40. FIEJ Communication Policy Resolution, June 4, 1976.

41. Nortamo, 11.

42. Francisco G. Labrado, "Presupuestos Ideologicos y Modalidades de la Ayuda Estatal a la Prensa," trans. Carlos Ruotolo, *Revista Espanola de la Opinion Publica* 30 (Octubre-Diciembre 1972): 12.

43. Freiberg, 171.

44. Labrado, 11.

45. International Commission for the Study of Communication Problems, 101.

46. G. William Domhoff, *The Powers That Be: Processes of Ruling Class Domination in America* (New York: Vintage Books, 1979), 24.

47. Joel Lewels, Jr., "The Newspaper Preservation Act," *Freedom of Information Center Report* no. 254 (January 1971): 5.

48. V. Lewis Bassie, "Subsidies," in David L. Sills, ed., *International Encyclopedia of the Social Sciences* (New York: Macmillan, 1968), 15: 366.

49. Colin Legum and John Cornwell, "Background Paper," in Twentieth Century Fund Task Force on the International Flow of News, *A Free and Balanced Flow* (Lexington, Mass.: Lexington Books, 1978), 54–55.

50. John Merrill and Harold Fisher, *The World's Great Dailies: Profiles of Fifty Newspapers* (New York: Hastings House, 1980), 311.

51. Einar Ostgaard, "Effects of Growing Dependence on Government Aid: Analysis of Official Reports Published in Norway and Sweden," *IPI Report* 25 (April 1976): 18.

52. Elise Burroughs, "Degree of Freedom Varies for 'Free Press,' " *Presstime* 4 (April 1982): 9.

53. Robert G. Picard, "Levels of State Intervention in the Western Press," *Mass Comm Review* 11 (Winter/Spring 1984): 27–35.

54. Robert G. Picard, "Patterns of State Intervention in Western Press Economics," *Journalism Quarterly* 62 (Spring 1985): 3–9.

55. Robert G. Picard, "Influences on State Intervention in Press Economics: A Regression Analysis" (Paper presented at the Western Communications Educators Conference, California State University, Fullerton, November 5, 1983).

56. Data sources included George Kurian, ed., *World Press Encyclopedia*, 2 vols. (New York: Facts on File, 1982); UNESCO, *World Communications* (New York: Unipub, 1975); UNESCO, *Statistical Yearbook* (New York: Unipub, 1982); and Anthony Smith, 1977.

6

Policies for the Future

Freedom is a sham as long as the best printing plants and huge stocks of paper are in the hands of the capitalists.
—Vladimir Ilyich Lenin[1]

To some observers press freedom is a simple concept. "It means that we are free to report and print information and opinions," says Robert W. Greene, assistant managing editor of *Newsday*.[2] Other observers, such as Ralph Lowenstein, see more complexities: "A completely free press is one in which newspapers, periodicals, news agencies, books, radio and television have absolute independence and critical ability, except for minimal libel and obscenity laws. The press has no concentrated ownership, marginal economic units or organized self-regulation."[3] Freedom of the press has been highly prized in the West because it is a vehicle for expression, the outward manifestation of self-consciousness by which democratic society is possible. Freedom of expression is necessary if the individual is to have the opportunity to act as a member of a society in which the individual's achievement and consciousness are prized.

In the Western world since the development of democratic forms of government, emphasis has been placed on freedom from government control. Independence of the press has been linked to commercialization of the industry and to the economic independence from government that presumably accom-

panied commercialization. This commercialization of the marketplace of ideas has received strong support, mainly from those
operating and profiting from private enterprises in that marketplace, and it has been linked to the concept of democracy
through the argument that the press better serves the public as
a private enterprise. One supporter of this view has argued:

It is . . . characteristic of a newspaper that it is only of any value to
the *individual* customer for *one* day. Thus the demand comes from a
market composed of a mass of individuals and will always do so. The
power of consumers is ideally distributed in an egalitarian manner,
which is what gives this area of the market its close affinity with *democracy* which cannot be cancelled out by any degree of concentration
of capital. The result is a public that "votes at the newsstand,"which
is an irrefutable sign of democracy, with however much assumed in-
tellectual superiority we may tend to regard it.[4]

As has been demonstrated, however, a private enterprise press
cannot, and should not, be equated with a free press, since private enterprises attempt to monopolize the marketplace and remove the opportunity for diverse viewpoints to be presented.
Mass communication is unavoidably influenced by society, which
exercises legal, political, economic, and social control over the
communication system. Even the relatively "free" societies such
as those of the Western world are influenced by the values,
policies, and needs of their societies and of those who control
the societies.

This viewpoint has gained increasing support in the twentieth century and provides an avenue for gaining a clearer view
of society and mass media, according to Theodore Peterson, Jay
Jenson, and William Rivers.[5] This "objective theory," as they
call it,

regards the media generally as comprising an institutional order whose
policy and behavior are determined by the dominant orders of society.
The media together, then, according to this theory, work on behalf of
the dominant orders as an agency of social control by manipulating
the pseudo-world which they convey and perpetuate.[6]

Most leftist social scientists embrace this theoretical perspective. They see communication as a political process and per-

ceive information as a resource that is subject to class control. In their view, capitalist classes use the media to perpetuate capitalist ideology, increase class control, and generally support class-differentiated society.

The simplistic concept that equates press freedom with "free" private enterprise is thus alien to objective theorists. Thomas McPhail epitomizes the rejection of any tie between the two when he writes:

The "free press" is basically a development press in favor of free enterprise and a capitalistic social system. The ideological role of the mass media in Western nations is to protect, perpetuate, and enlarge the role and influence of the capitalistic system in all phases of decision making . . . the Western press is a development press and has, in fact, successfully developed itself into an ideological arm of the capitalistic and free enterprise system. In essence it provides free and paid for (via advertising) support of a social and political system consistent with basically maintaining the status quo.[7]

Christopher Lasch has also noted this process, but argues that the mass media reinforce the status quo

not by disseminating an authoritarian ideology of patriotism, militarism, and submission, as so many left-wing critics assume, but by destroying collective memory, by replacing accountable authority with a new kind of star system, and by treating all ideas, all political programs, all controversies and disagreements as equally newsworthy, equally deserving of fitful attention, and therefore equally inconsequential and forgettable.[8]

The concept that the free press equals a private, commercial press is also challenged by arguments about private economic power and its effects on communication. This view was typified by the Council of Europe when it contended, "Freedom of the press cannot be governed by the rules of free enterprise alone."[9] Even in the United States, those whose views are far from the left rarely deny that the marketplace of ideas is increasingly falling under the economic control of large commercial interests. Charles Ferris, former chairman of the Federal Communications Commission, recently observed: "It is now becoming clear that free speech can be surrendered to market pressures as easily as it can be subverted by government. To-day, commercial competition for the broadest possible audi-ence has stilled divergent voices and left us with the monotone of commonly held values and viewpoints."[10]

Others who share more critical views of capitalism see com-mercialization of the marketplace as inevitably destroying all possibilities for the diversity of voices necessary for democracy. Tom Kent, chairman of the Royal Commission on Newspapers (Canada), argues:

Where a newspaper has become merely one business among others, the point of tradeoff shifts heavily against the public responsibility and towards profit. Under the mechanism of the business system, that process is bound to continue to the bitter end because the people who are prepared to look at newspapers that way (as profit making enter-prise) can always pay more for them than the people who are going to look at them as a public responsibility.[11]

Concentration of ownership and newspaper mortality have visibly reduced the number of independent and competing newspapers throughout the Western world. These develop-ments have reduced the outlets for diverse views, outlets that are necessary for the free operation of the marketplace of ideas. Proponents of the "free press through private enterprise" ar-gument contend that the public makes choices in the market-place and thus determines which media and, consequently, which ideas survive. But when economic activities and busi-ness decisions made for the sake of profit reduce and restrict the products in the marketplace, freedom of choice is denied the reader. This development is just as devastating to press freedom as government restriction of unorthodox viewpoints.

Robert Cirino has noted that the little competition left in the marketplace is exploited by the commercial media in order to mask their continuing efforts to monopolize the marketplace and to provide the appearance of diversity:

A major propaganda success of the communications industry is con-vincing the American people that there is a fierce competition among news agencies. There is a fierce competition all right, but it is to make a larger profit or audience, not to compete in the realm of ideas or concepts in news coverage and presentation. . . . The media owners will do anything to maintain these myths. They will spend millions to cover live a presidential trip or a moon shot or a sporting event. They may even search out a new controversial topic if it will help them maintain their myths and earn prestige. They will do anything to keep the public from realizing that the establishment dominates society through its direct and indirect control of the nation's communication system.[12]

Patrick Parsons, in his Marxian analysis of newspaper economics, has also criticized the view that press competition revolves around diversity. Newspaper readers do not decide what shall triumph in the marketplace, he argues, because the real market commercial newspapers seek is not readers but advertisers. The commercial marketplace for ideas is thus very different from the commercial marketplace for goods. While most industries sell primarily to a consuming public, newspapers get most of their revenue from other businesses (through advertising) and thus depend upon ad placement and economic decisions of other businesses.[13]

It is generally accepted that economic control of the marketplace for goods is an unhealthy development, and even the nations most vigorously supporting the capitalist system regulate such control through antitrust mechanisms. Economic control of the marketplace of ideas is equally unhealthy, but many people do not readily accept the argument that the state must combat such control. It is suprising that there are separate approaches to the two markets, since economic control of the marketplace for goods is far less damaging to democracy than control of the marketplace for ideas.

Those who have criticized the Western press through objective theory and economic control arguments have themselves been the subject of criticism from other, more critical, social theorists. Kaarle Nordenstreng has noted that their studies are generally guided by "half-way approaches" to communication research (i.e., the study of economic structure and content). These approaches do not provide a sufficient basis for research because they do not offer a "conceptually comprehensive theory of socio-economic process."[14] I have attempted to avoid that weakness by presenting communication as an integral part of democratic society and exploring how Western nations have attempted to change the nature of mass communication by providing the means for the press to be more responsive to social needs. These efforts have altered the traditional adversarial relationship between press and state. This study has shown the changes to be linked to democratic socialism—a subtle, sophisticated, and ethical approach to modern democracy.

Democratic socialism provides a conceptually comprehensive theory of socioeconomic processes, based on expanding the role of the individual in democratic society and providing real freedom of choice. Erich Fromm has argued:

The future of democracy depends on the realization of the individualism that has been the ideological aim of modern thought since the Renaissance. . . . The victory of freedom is possible only if democracy develops into a society in which the individual, his growth and happiness, is the aim and purpose of culture, in which life does not need any justification in success or anything else, and in which the individual is not subordinated to or manipulated by any power outside himself, be it the State or the economic machine; finally, a society in which his conscience and ideals are not the internalization of external demands, but are really *his* and express the aims that result from the peculiarity of his self.[15]

The emergence of such a democracy will require a revolution in the way knowledge is controlled in society. As Michael Harrington has observed, this revolution is necessary for the individual to be aware of and to understand what is occurring in the world about him and to make informed choices and decisions.[16]

If society is to expand the democratic participation of its members, original, critical thought must be promoted, and public opinion cannot be manipulated by mass media that are intentionally or tacitly controlled by economic and social elites. The lack of access and diversity hampers democratic progress, as does the increasing trivialization of social and political reporting for the sake of profit. *The Progressive* recently lamented the passing of, and the media coverage of, what little political debate has occurred in the United States: "Clearly the mass media, on which

we all must depend to some extent, have lost all sense of politics as the way we pursue the common purposes that shape our
lives. By cheapening the very meaning of politics, they help
ensure our continuing subservience to bureaucratic manipulation by the elites that hold sway in our society."[17]

In response to such concerns, democratic socialist views have
appeared increasingly in the discussion of the relationship between the press and society. This discussion has attempted to
blend these views in order to postulate a comprehensive democratic socialist theory of the press, a theory that answers Kaarle
Nordenstreng's criticisms of recent communication research but,
admittedly, one that is probably not radical enough to meet his
approval.

When the social responsibility theory was postulated in the
late 1940s, its proponents argued that media should voluntarily
accept the "burdens" of behaving in the best interest of society, rather than in their own narrow economic and political interests. If the press did not behave responsibly, the Hutchins
Commission warned, the state would soon step in to compel
the press to serve society's interests. This study has shown how
Western nations intervene increasingly in press economics to
try to protect social interests. In much of the Western world
during the late 1960s and early 1970s, the social responsibility
theory of the press, which is based upon self-control and ethical behavior, gave way, often unnoticed, to the democratic socialist theory of the press. Instead of relying upon the press to
promote the public good, this new approach put the protection
and promotion of the public good in the public's hands through
the mechanisms of the state.

Like the libertarian and social responsibility theories, the
democratic socialist theory is a normative theory. In other words,
it does not merely describe the press and how it operates, but
presents a clear view of what the press *should* be and what it
should do. Under this view of the relationship between the press
and society, press freedom no longer means merely the right
to publish but also the public's right to have access to the press
and to a full accounting of the events and opinions of society.
Because the people are viewed as the basis of society and governance, the press must be democratized—like the political sys-

tem—if democracy is to survive and expand. State intervention in press economics has been continuous since the early development of newspapers in Europe; but the amounts and degrees of intervention changed as democratic rule emerged, economic needs of the press changed, and the different modern government economic policies developed.

Jean Seaton has noted that since the press became independent of overt, coercive, and disruptive government economic control, "governments have seen the press as an industry of such exceptional political importance that during this century they have made a policy of having no policy for it at all."[18] Though true to some extent, this statement represents a simplistic view of the situation. Western governments throughout most of this century have pursued economic policies toward the press that favored large, commercial press entities over their smaller counterparts. It seems reasonable to assume that these policies are related to the disputed economic view that supporting commercial entities benefits society in the long run.

In the United States, for instance, the government has made regular forays into the public policy arena, dealing with such matters as advertising, privacy, defamation, and state support for the newspaper industry. These policies have been consistently pursued by the legislative and executive branches regardless of whether "liberals" or "conservatives" have controlled those branches of government. The keystone of these policies is strong support for private ownership of communications media, a philosophy that has led to an increase in monopolies in the print media and a concurrent growth of communications conglomerates. A second aspect of the policy has been that the government should make little direct intervention, but that growth and economic health in the industry should be promoted through tax and other advantages. A third aspect of U.S. policy toward the press has been government inattention to the social costs of growth in the newspaper industry, an inattention undoubtedly promoted by the view that all types of economic growth are beneficial to society. As a result, the government has not supported or promoted diversity, political ideology, or controversy in the print media. The structural inequities that have afflicted the press and its use by the public have

been tacitly accepted as normal for a commercial press in a capitalist "democracy."

In recent years, as Western states have moved steadily into
economic planning and intervention involving the press, two
major social perspectives have emerged. The first is the pan-
European view of the necessity of various degrees of government intervention. The second view, primarily accepted in the
United States, maintains strong opposition to such intervention. Roland Homet, Jr. has noted the different approaches in
his recent study of communication policymaking in Western
nations, a study that focuses on telecommunications but applies to the print media as well. "American reliance on market
forces is based on a populist distrust of government, just as European reliance on government control (especially in broadcasting) is anchored in a concern to protect the cultural patrimony
from business exploitation."[19]

The diminishing of political activity by surviving European
newspapers has also encouraged European press intervention.
As Anthony Smith notes:

In many countries there was alarm because the press was failing to
perform its traditional task of sustaining ideological debate in politics.
Newspapers found that their political allegiances in many cases re-
pelled rather than attracted new readers and advertisers. During the
1960s Europeans became tired of the traditional slogans of left and right
and, most important, advertisers needed to reach the new nonpolitical
mass audience—young couples building their homes for the first time,
high-wage earners. The audiences of politics and the audiences of
newspapers, hitherto synchronous, now began to be pried apart. The
younger, highly political public of the later 1960s found little in the
daily newspaper to charm them, only a reaffirmation of their hostility
toward the system. As a result, many European countries began a plan
to organize governmental subsidies to the press in order to preserve
the linkages between daily newspapers and specific blocks of opinion.[20]

The press has long supported state intervention on both sides
of the Atlantic, with publishers' and journalists' groups regularly supporting intervention through advantages and indirect
subsidies. But the new intervention of the second half of the

twentieth century has not increased or protected profits. Rather, it has directly affected the profit-making capabilities of major newspapers.

Clyde Slade has noted that in the United States, newspaper publishers have long viewed freedom of the press as having two functions. First, it means that Congress may not make laws that could control the press, and second, that "Congress shall make a lot of laws to foster its privileged status."[21] Thus, suggestions for regulating or controlling competition and access and for supporting a true marketplace of ideas have been met with hostility because they challenged both aspects of the publishers' view of press freedom. Similar conflicts arose in Europe as modern forms of intervention were proposed and instituted. The nations that early instituted new subsidies and advantages were able to overcome the objections mainly because the commercial, profit-making press represented a minority interest among publishers, and press associations and trade groups did not present a common voice of opposition.

Other dangers identified in these discussions of intervention, particulary subsidization, were 1) unequal distribution of aid because of political favoritism, 2) coercive use of aid to gain acquiescence and cooperation with the government in power, 3) dependence on funds to the point that removal of aid would immediately halt publication, 4) the possibility that future legislatures could alter regulations of impartiality, 5) the possibility that aid could subsidize incompetent management, 6) removal of any incentive to improve financial conditions of newspapers, and 7) removal of incentives to improve newspaper quality. The nations choosing to increase their intervention with direct subsidies were aware of the potential dangers. Even publishers and politicians supporting aid noted the problems and required the institution of safeguards. The prospect of discriminatory government practices that might lead to economic control by government prompted legislation providing strict administrative procedures that would nearly eliminate the possibility of such control.

In choosing to take the risks of such intervention, the press and the state in these countries accepted arguments that political control through such activity would be difficult to pursue because it would be obvious and would raise immediate and harsh criticism that could quickly halt all intervention. Further, the only intervention that newspapers would be compelled to accept was regulation, which did not seem to concern many supporters of press freedom to the extent that direct subsidies did.

As early as 1923, Lucy Maynard Salmon noted that bribery through subsidies is not a very effective control in the Western world, and such views may have helped calm criticism of modern subsidization. Salmon argued: "In its most seductive form, control of the press has been secured by the favors shown it. . . . Instances of a direct effort to control the press through bribery and corruption are less numerous and also less effective than are the more insidious means of which the press itself may be unconscious."[22] Drawing on the French experience, J. W. Freiberg in 1981 reflected a similar view, saying that financial aid is the "most minimally coercive form of state intervention in the press."[23] Such views, held mainly in Europe, helped allay fears of the dangers of subsidies and other intervention, and helped lead to the modern forms of state intervention in the press. The dangers of subsidizing incompetence and removing incentives for improvement were addressed in some intervention programs by providing cutoff dates and including requirements concerning what the aid could be used for.

Any study of intervention is fraught with political overtones, for all political, social, and economic policies are inherently ideological. Conservatives and liberals, for instance, use the study of intervention as a means of showing how government denies what they perceive as the right to private property; Marxists use the study of intervention to show the amount of subsidy to capital and to the infrastructure that benefits private enterprise and political control. From the first perspective, the most significant intervention—i.e., that which denies or limits the use of private property—is price and ownership regulation. Such regulation is a contradiction of bourgeois thought about private property, yet regulation exists even in the most market-oriented Western nations. The highest level of such regulation, of course, is found in the nations that restrict competition in the press and in other industries as well. Proponents of the conservative economic view also see grants and subsidies as a denial of private property because such aid is not usually available to all newspapers. This aid also interferes with the ability of some newspaper owners, especially the owners of the largest press firms, to pursue policies with their properties that damage the property of others by placing those enterprises at a competitive disadvantage.

Clearly, state intervention in press economics, particularly through advantages, reduces the cost of operations through fiscal advantages, provides capital for improvements, provides funds through cash subsidies and advertising, and regulates or does not regulate various fiscal aspects of the industry. Most conservatives and liberals do not view advantages as damaging to property, since they support the use of capital and private property for the pursuit of profit. Those nations that provide loan programs and grants and subsidies to meet the operational expenses of the privately owned press provide even stronger subsidies to capital than do nations that rely mainly upon advantages. The strongest subsidies to capital are found in the Welfare Capitalist and Capitalism Augmentor nations, despite the significant influence of socialist ideologies. It must be noted, however, that such subsidization is not given solely to guarantee profits, but also to meet social needs.

Left-wing social scientists recognize that the role of the Western state in economics is becoming more intimate, and the socialist and communist parties of Western Europe have generally accepted the view that capitalism can be combatted not only by revolution but by the democratic process. Their policy, therefore, has been to attempt to control government through the ballot box and then to control capitalism with state apparatuses. The parties have been influential in the area of press policy by using their political strength to help wrest some economic control out of the hands of private owners and place it within more publicly responsive apparatuses.

Modern state intervention in press economics generally parallels the basic macroeconomic policies pursued by Western nations, many of which have been influenced by socialist and communist parties. The five patterns of intervention discussed in Chapter 5 closely approximate the major approaches to general economic policy in the Western world. No important differences between macroeconomic policy and press intervention policy have been found.

In the United States, government policy in the area of press politics is best explored in terms of what Alan Wolfe calls "growth politics." According to this ideology, the two dominant political parties came to an ideological agreement that industrial growth would be the primary political emphasis in post–World War II America.[24] Wolfe describes this ideology as being manifested in the belief that business is the source of all growth and improvement in living conditions, and that business and industry should be supported and aided by government policy. He maintains that the promotion of private economic health has become the single major focus of government policies and that government spending programs, subsidies, and indirect aid are used to promote private sector growth. His thesis applies well to state intervention in press economics, where support for large communications concerns has been emphasized—especially support for newspaper chains and communications conglomerates. The state has intervened with tax advantages, regulatory relief, and other fiscal advantages and subsidies that support such firms.

Despite the fact that general policies toward state intervention in press economics exist in the United States, there has never been a comprehensive study of the needs, purposes, and impact of such intervention. Unlike the governments of the majority of other Western nations, the U.S. government has never commissioned and completed significant studies of press economics and state intervention. Thus the United States does not have policies that emphasize the press's value to democratic society and outline how government spending, subsidies, and fiscal advantages could be used to promote this value. Instead, the general macroeconomic policies followed for all industries, with a few special interest policies haphazardly thrown in, are used by the government in its intervention in press economics.

The lack of comprehensive intervention policies for all industries, not merely for the newspaper industry, has drawn increasing criticism from observers. Arguments that intervention must be reviewed and undertaken for specific purposes deemed beneficial to society are being heard more often. Without such studies and the establishment of intervention principles, the public good suffers. An example of ill-advised intervention in newspaper economics is seen in the monopoly sector of the press, where the Newspaper Preservation Act—one of the most conspicuous examples of special interest legislation—exempts some newspapers from antitrust provisions. To the detriment of other media and of consumers, this act allows some newspapers to operate together and to engage in price fixing and other activities normally prohibited by U.S. antitrust legislation.

Similarly, general business tax policies are applied to the newspaper industry and thus favor growth through the acquisition of newspapers by chains and conglomerates. Significant tax advantages accrue to companies that acquire additional newspapers. Independent newspaper owners often find themselves forced to sell inherited papers in order to pay estate taxes, because such laws base taxes on "fair market values" that newspaper chains have created and only newspaper chains can afford.

The U.S. government makes almost no direct or specific intervention in press economics through cash grants, subsidies, or loans to help the press modernize or acquire new facilities and equipment. Instead, it pursues policies that promote general conditions assumed to be conducive to the health of the entire industry. Its most extensive policies involve the use of tax incentives to encourage reinvestment and growth. In practice, however, these policies discourage independent ownership and reduce employment through the creation of economies of scale in the industry, since they are not formulated to preserve media plurality by aiding the most needy press enterprises.

The most interventionistic assistance is provided through postal rate reductions and government advertising. Although postal rate advantages have been reduced, they still account for significant reductions in operating costs for some papers. Government advertising is also important to newspapers, since it requires little effort from advertising sales departments and brings substantial revenue to many newspapers; but such advertising dollars generally go to the most established units of the press and thus do nothing to improve the economic health of smaller papers.

The breadth of U.S. government involvement in press economics has escaped the notice of many American critics of European intervention. At least two dozen types of intervention have been documented.[25] If these critics of state intervention truly believed that intervention was harmful, they would be casting a more critical eye at the situation in this country. One suspects, however, that they are not critical of the U.S. situation because it supports the infrastructures of corporatist, commercially based industry and helps make the newspaper industry one of the most profitable industries in the United States.

If there is no significant difference between existing macroeconomic policies and press intervention policies in Western nations, one must ask why intervention as a whole has been so feared and scrutinized. The answer, of course, involves the special relationship between the press and democratic rule. The problems of newspaper mortality, concentration of ownership, and diminishing access—and the attendant control provided media owners and operators by these changes in the marketplace—provided the ammunition necessary for democratic socialists to argue that the press must be viewed and regulated more like other commercially based industries if freedom was to be preserved, in some form, in the marketplace of ideas.

Thus, just as democratic socialist views of economics have influenced European government policies in economics generally, the new intervention in press economics is a result of the extension of such views to press economics. Under the argument that the press should not be left to pursue its own course and ignore social needs any more than other industries should be allowed to make economic and social decisions without societal supervision and control, proponents of democratic socialist views have broken down barriers to intervention in press economics.

Intervention in the marketplaces of both ideas and goods and services has clearly been instituted to ameliorate the harmful effects of capitalism. Modern intervention in press economics, however, has been made not only to halt undesirable behavior in the marketplace, but to provide means by which the desirable behavior (i.e., diversity and democratic participation) may develop or survive. The recognition of the press's special role in democracy is an important way in which press intervention differs from general economic intervention.

While Western nations may agree on the need to intervene in the newspaper industry, this study has shown that there is no agreement on how intervention should be undertaken. Two distinct courses—regulation and subsidization—have been pursued by nations most concerned with the effects of commercialization and monopolization of the marketplace on political activity. It remains to be seen which of the two is most effective at preserving a diverse and free marketplace of ideas. Other nations have generally chosen to rely on the marketplace and to promote newspaper interests through fiscal advantages. The problems of concentration of ownership, newspaper mortality, and continuing rejections of political roles for the press persist in those nations.

PRINCIPLES AND POLICIES FOR THE FUTURE

It appears that in the foreseeable future the various forms of intervention in press economics will continue throughout the Western world. No significant suggestions for reducing intervention have been made in the nations with the heaviest intervention, and suggestions for increasing intervention are being offered more frequently in nations that do not strongly regulate or subsidize the press today. In Canada, for instance, the Kent Commission in 1981 proposed strengthening cartel regulations and providing subsidies to marginal units of the press.[26] Charles Novitz, president of the Society of Professional Journalists/SDX, recently suggested in his organization's national magazine that U.S. intervention be increased. "Churches, political groups, and individuals have subsidized publications since the press was invented. So, in the face of lost jobs and lost voices, should we finally consider the 'unthinkable'—an outright subsidy to those engaged in news pursuits?" He answered his question by suggesting increased intervention.[27]

As long as the marketplace of ideas is controlled by undemocratic economic activities, democracy cannot survive even

in its present form, much less move closer to its idealized form.
Even under the best conditions democracy has proved to be a
fragile commodity; with a commercialized, economically controlled press, it can be dashed to pieces just as if it were crushed
by dictatorship. State intervention in the commercial marketplace is not the final solution for the difficulties posed to democratic participation in society. Clearly, even the slightest intervention made for the purpose of repairing the damage of
economic competition will require additional intervention to
compensate for further damage. Increasing intervention must
ultimately force citizens of democratic societies to change the
way they view the relationship between the state and the press,
says Anthony Smith:

We are seeing a single complex of institutions, private, public and
mixed, evolving in modern societies as mediators of information and
entertainment, mutually dependent, mutually abrasive, with func-
tional overlaps and newly emerging demarcations. There is thus a kind
of cultural-informational complex growing at the heart of modern societies, which does not in itself spell any kind of doom but which pro-
foundly alters the way in which we should think about the role of the
government and the press.[28]

This study has attempted to provide a modern democratic
framework within which to contemplate the changing nature of
press-state relations. It has also provided a proposal, implicit in
the democratic socialist hierarchy of press freedom, for seeking
a more democratic approach to the role of the press in society.
I do not suggest that the intervention patterns practiced in
Western Europe be immediately transferred to the United States,
nor that all Western European intervention supports the goal
of wider public participation. I do not believe that the democratic socialist approach could be fully implemented in the United
States. The European newspaper industries and political ideologies differ so greatly from those in the United States that it
would be ludicrous to expect that European solutions and political forms would solve the problems of our press and meet
with the approval of U.S. citizens.

This does not mean that the democratic socialist approach has nothing to offer and cannot be pursued in the United States. Despite anti-socialist rhetoric in this country, it is clear that socialism has permeated and tempered American capitalism, with much change resulting from the populist, progressive, and socialist movements of the early twentieth century. The ideals, values, and rhetoric generated by these movements and nurtured by liberals and progressives through the rest of the century have created a potential for adoption of elements of the democratic socialist approach to the press. Arguments to improve access, to reduce monopoly and concentration in the press and broadcasting, to improve the quality of information carried, to reduce owner control, and to democratize management have been made by individuals from a wide variety of ideological backgrounds. Much of their concern and many of their suggestions for action have coincided, often unbeknownst to these advocates, with democratic socialist viewpoints. There is great opportunity to promote the democratic socialist approach and to introduce its principles into public media policy in the United States. It is not unrealistic to expect that some principles and forms of European intervention could be imported, since some of the desires of democratic socialists are already supported in the United States and do not conflict with the prevailing public ideology.

The major principle that should be accepted is that multiple newspapers are needed throughout the nation to meet the need for diversity in viewpoints and coverage presented. The second principle that needs to be accepted is that the government should encourage and assist such plurality by pursuing supportive intervention policies. The third principle is support for independent ownership of newspapers. In practice, such principles could be supported by charging higher tax rates on the profits of corporations owning multiple newspapers, by limiting the number of newspapers that a company or individual may own, by removing tax advantages arising from the acquisition of newspapers, and by removing or reducing inheritance taxes on independently owned newspapers.

Postal rate advantages could also be reduced for newspapers owned by chains or conglomerates, and such advantages could be increased for independently owned papers—especially small

rural or neighborhood newspapers. Grants and loans to promote capital improvements for small independent papers should
be made available, perhaps through the Small Business Administration. Cooperative ownership of printing facilities by small
papers, especially weeklies, should be encouraged; and exemptions from antitrust provisions should be sought to enable more
cooperation in advertising sales, supply acquisition, capital acquisition, and other functions of such independent papers.
Government advertising should be redirected to help smaller
papers. Publication of required legal advertising could be mandated in the smaller independent papers, and government
agencies could place their advertising so as to favor the independent press.

Groups with diverse ideological and political viewpoints
should be encouraged to express their views, and avenues for
such expression should be opened. Access to the pages of
newspapers could be required of existing newspapers in exchange for advantages and subsidies, or be made available by
the government or some quasi-governmental agency through the
purchase of newspaper space. Political and social groups should
be encouraged and helped in starting not-for-profit newspapers to carry information and opinion. Significant advantages
and subsidies should be made available for such media, perhaps by removing some subsidies and advantages from the
largest newspaper chains and communication conglomerates.

While this study has focused on newspapers, the question of
democratizing communication also applies to broadcasting and
other information sources. The growth and potential of electronic communication capabilities have been seen as a technological means of increasing diversity, but broadcasters have never
shown a proclivity toward conveying ideas or debate in a manner that can even begin to answer the basic requirements of a
marketplace for ideas. If broadcasting and information sources
are to serve the democratic needs of society, even greater changes
are needed in their structures and operation than are needed
in the newspaper industry.

Under true democracy, society belongs to the people, but an
approximation of the ideal can be achieved only if society's institutions—especially those that so strongly influence culture—

The Press and the Decline of Democracy

operate in such a way as to promote a fuller democracy. The press no longer serves the basic democratic purpose that it did at the dawn of democracy. Western nations, including many of those with extensive intervention in the press today, are faced with two choices: continuing their course toward a technocratic and monopolistic press industry that exhibits little concern for social needs, or embarking on an uncharted and uncertain journey that holds out the promise of a more egalitarian society.

The tension between having a free press and having state involvement in the press to promote democracy is merely another facet of the democratic tension between liberty and equality. The struggle to democratize the press is a microcosm of the struggle to democratize society. Society must strive to achieve maximum press freedom while at the same time striving to provide its citizens with equal access to the press. Western states have made great strides in removing governmental restrictions and threats to the press, and thus provide the world with a good example of freedom from such restraints. But equality of access to the press has steadily eroded in the past two centuries because of new controls—mainly economic—that have arisen to impede freedom of expression. Similarly, democratic participation and control have not matured. The internal and structural restrictions on press liberty are as damaging to the maturation of democracy as external restrictions were to democratic development. If internal, structural restraints are not modified, liberty will continue to erode as the content of the media is homogenized and elite rule perpetuated.

An accommodation between the liberty needed by the press to operate as a vehicle for ideas and the public's need for equality to express and receive ideas must be reached. Without such a reconciliation, structural control of information and expression will continue, and the furtherance of democratic governance will be hindered. Public policies can either restrict or aid the press in carrying out its goals. Some Western nations have begun to use their policies to balance liberty and equality in the press, in order to achieve a higher level of democratic rule. This healthy development should not go unnoticed by those concerned about the state of the press in the United States today.

NOTES

1. V. I. Lenin, *Selected Works* (New York: International Publishers, 1919), 7: 226–227.
2. Robert W. Greene, "The Media and Democratic Society" (Address at the Fourth Estate Awards Banquet, School of Journalism and Mass Communication, University of Iowa, Iowa City, March 8, 1980).
3. Ralph Lowenstein, "Measuring World Press Freedom as a Political Indicator" (Ph.D. diss., University of Missouri-Columbia, 1967), 45.
4. Joseph H. Kaiser, *Press Planning: The State and Newspaper Publishing in Germany* (Zurich: International Press Institute, 1975), 19.
5. Theodore B. Peterson, Jay W. Jenson, and William L. Rivers, *The Mass Media and Modern Society* (New York: Holt, Rinehart and Winston, 1965).
6. Ibid., 122.
7. Thomas L. McPhail, *Electronic Colonialism: The Future of International Broadcasting and Communication* (Beverly Hills, Calif.: Sage Publications, 1981), 24.
8. Christopher Lasch, "Mass Culture Revisited," *democracy* 1 (October 1981): 19.
9. Council of Europe, Resolution 834 (1978).
10. Charles Ferris (Address to the Academy of Television Arts and Sciences, Los Angeles, May 1, 1979).
11. Barrie Zeicker, "Reflections on the Kent Commission," *Content* (January/February 1982): 7.
12. Robert Cirino, *Don't Blame the People* (New York: Vintage Books, 1971), 221.
13. Patrick Parsons, "Economics of the Newspaper Industry: A Marxian Analysis" (M.A. thesis, California State University, Northridge, 1978), 237–238.
14. Kaarle Nordenstreng, "Recent Developments in European Communications Theory," *Journal of Communication* 2 (Winter 1977): 41–50.
15. Erich Fromm, *Escape from Freedom* (New York: Rinehart and Co., 1941), 270–271.
16. Michael Harrington, *Toward a Democratic Left* (New York: Macmillan, 1968), 111.
17. "The Sporting Life," *The Progressive* (January 1983): 11.
18. Jean Seaton, "Government Policy and the Mass Media," in James Curran, ed., *The British Press: A Manifesto* (London: Macmillan Press, 1978), 300–301.
19. Ronald S. Homet, Jr., *Politics, Cultures and Communication: Euro-*

pean vs. American Approaches to Communications Policymaking (New York: Praeger Special Studies, 1979), 99.

20. Anthony Smith, *Goodbye Gutenberg* (New York: Oxford University Press, 1980), 43–44.

21. Clyde Slade, "Daily Newspapers and Social Accountability," *Journal of Communication Inquiry* 5 (Winter 1980): 49.

22. Lucy Maynard Salmon, *The Newspaper and Authority* (New York: Oxford University Press, 1923), 146.

23. J. W. Freiberg, *The French Press: Class, State and Ideology* (New York: Praeger, 1981), 69.

24. Alan Wolfe, *America's Impasse: The Rise and Fall of the Politics of Growth* (New York: Pantheon Books, 1981).

25. Robert G. Picard, "State Intervention in U.S. Press Economics," *Gazette* 30 (1982): 3–11.

26. *Report of the Royal Commission on Newspapers* (Hull, Quebec: Canadian Government Publishing Centre, 1981).

27. Charles Novitz, "Is It Time for a News Subsidy?" *The Quill* 70 (October 1982): 29.

28. Anthony Smith, "State Intervention and the Management of the Press," in James Curran, ed., *The British Press: A Manifesto* (London: Macmillan Press, 1978), 53–72.

Bibliography

BOOKS

Alford, Robert R. "Paradigms of Relations between State and Society." In *Stress and Contradiction in Modern Capitalism*, ed. L. Linberg. Lexington, Mass.: Lexington Books, 1976.

Altschull, J. Herbert. *Agents of Power*. New York: Longman, 1984.

American Institute for Political Communication. *Media Monopoly and Politics*. Washington, D.C.: American Institute for Political Communication, 1973.

Andrain, Charles F. *Politics and Economic Policy in Western Democracies*. North Scituate, Mass.: Duxbury Press, 1980.

Aronson, James. *Packaging the News: A Critical Survey of Press, Radio, TV*. New York: International Publishers, 1971.

Aspinall, Arthur. *Politics and the Press, 1780–1850*. New York: Barnes and Noble, 1974.

Baker, Leonard. *The Guaranteed Society*. New York: Macmillan, 1968.

Banks, Arthur S., ed. *Political Handbook of the World: 1978*. New York: McGraw-Hill, 1978.

Barron, Jerome. *Freedom of the Press for Whom? The Rise of Access to Mass Media*. Bloomington, Ind.: Indiana University Press, 1973.

Benenson, Peter. *A Free Press*. London: The Fabian Society, 1961.

Berlin, Isaiah. *Four Essays on Liberty*. New York: Oxford University Press, 1970.

———. *Two Concepts of Liberty*. Oxford: Clarendon Press, 1958.

Bernstein, Eduard. *Evolutionary Socialism*. Trans. Edith C. Harvey. New York: Schocken Books, 1961.

Bird, George L., and Merwin, Frederick E., eds. *The Newspaper and Society*. New York: Prentice-Hall, 1942.

Bleyer, Willard G. *Main Currents in the History of American Journalism*. Boston: Houghton Mifflin, 1927.

Boorstin, Daniel. *The Americans: The Colonial Experience*. New York: Random House, 1958.

Bottomore, Tom. *Political Sociology*. New York: Harper and Row, 1979.

Boyce, George; Curran, James; and Wingate, Pauline, eds. *Newspaper History*. Beverly Hills, Calif.: Sage Publications, 1978.

Brigham, Clarence. *History and Bibliography of American Newspapers, 1690–1829*. 2 vols. Worcester, Mass.: American Antiquarian Society, 1947.

Brucker, Herbert. *Communication Is Power*. New York: Oxford University Press, 1973.

———. *Freedom of Information*. New York: Macmillan, 1951.

Carnoy, Martin, and Shearer, Derek. *Economic Democracy: The Challenge of the 1980s*. White Plains, N.Y.: M. E. Sharpe, 1980.

Carrillo, Santiago. *Eurocommunism and the State*. Westport, Conn.: Lawrence Hill and Co., 1978.

Carson, Robert B.; Ingles, Jerry; and McLaud, Douglas, eds. *Government in the American Economy*. Lexington, Mass.: D. C. Heath, 1973.

Chafee, Zachariah, Jr. *Government and Mass Communication*. 2 vols. Chicago: University of Chicago Press, 1947.

Cirino, Robert. *Don't Blame the People*. New York: Vintage Books, 1971.

Clor, Harry, ed. *The Mass Media and Modern Democracy*. Chicago: Rand McNally College Publishing Co., 1974.

Commission on Freedom of the Press. *A Free and Responsible Press*. Chicago: University of Chicago Press, 1947.

Curran, James. "The Press as an Agency of Social Control." In *Newspaper History*, ed. George Boyce, J. Curran, and P. Wingate, 51–75. Beverly Hills, Calif.: Sage Publications, 1978.

Curran, James, ed. *The British Press: A Manifesto*. London: Macmillan Press, 1978.

Curran, James; Gurevitch, M.; and Woollacott, J., eds. *Mass Communication and Society*. Beverly Hills, Calif.: Sage Publications, 1979.

Curran, James, and Seaton, Jean. *Power without Responsibility: The Press and Broadcasting in Britain*. Douglas, Isle of Man: Fontana Paperbacks, 1981.

Dahl, Folke, ed. *The Birth of the European Press*. Stockholm: The Royal Library, 1960.

Dahl, Robert A. *A Preface to Democratic Theory*. Chicago: University of Chicago Press, 1965.

———. *Dilemmas of Pluralist Democracy*. New Haven: Yale University Press, 1982.

Denitch, Bogdan, ed. *Democratic Socialism: The Mass Left in Advanced Industrial Societies.* Totowa, N.J.: Allanheld, Osmun and Co., 1981.

Domhoff, G. William. *The Powers That Be: Processes of Ruling Class Domination in America.* New York: Vintage Books, 1979.

Dordick, Herbert S.; Bradley, Helen G.; and Nanus, Burt. *The Emerging Network Marketplace.* Norwood, N.J.: Ablex Publishing Co., 1981.

Durbin, Evan. *The Politics of Democratic Socialism.* London: Routledge and Kegan Paul, 1940.

Emerson, Thomas I. *The System of Freedom of Expression.* New York: Random House, 1970.

Emery, Edwin. *The Press and America.* 3rd ed. Englewood Cliffs, N.J.: Prentice-Hall, 1972.

The Europa Yearbook: A World Survey. 2 vols. London: Europa Publications, 1981.

Farrar, Roland T., and Stevens, John D. *Mass Media and the National Experience.* New York: Harper and Row, 1971.

Freiberg, J. W. *The French Press: Class, State and Ideology.* New York: Praeger, 1981.

Friedenberg, Edgar Z. *The Disposal of Liberty and Other Industrial Wastes.* Garden City, N.Y.: Doubleday, 1975.

Friedrich, Carl J., and Brezezinski, Zbigniew K. *Totalitarian Dictatorship and Autocracy.* 2nd ed. Cambridge, Mass.: Harvard University Press, 1965.

Fromm, Erich. *Escape from Freedom.* New York: Rinehart and Co., 1941.

Gans, Herbert J. *Deciding What's News.* New York: Pantheon Books, 1979.

Gay, Peter. *The Dilemma of Democratic Socialism.* New York: Columbia University Press, 1952.

Gustafsson, Karl Erik, and Hadenius, Stig. *Swedish Press Policy.* Stockholm: The Swedish Institute, 1976.

Habermas, Jürgen. *Communication and the Evolution of Society.* Boston: Beacon Press, 1978.

Hachten, William. *The World News Prism: Changing Media, Clashing Ideologies.* Ames, Iowa: Iowa State University Press, 1981.

Harrington, Michael. *Decade of Decision: The Crisis of the American System.* New York: Simon and Schuster, 1980.

———. *Socialism.* New York: Saturday Review Press, 1972.

———. *Toward a Democratic Left.* New York: Macmillan, 1968.

———. *The Twilight of Capitalism.* New York: Simon and Schuster, 1976.

Heinberg, Aage, ed. *Scandinavia Past and Present.* 3 vols. Arnkrone, Denmark: Eduard Henriksen, 1959.

Hirsh, Fred, and Gordon, David. *Newspaper Money*. London: Hutch-
    inson, 1978.
Hocking, William E. *Freedom of the Press: A Framework of Principle*. Chi-
    cago: University of Chicago Press, 1947.
Hohenberg, John. *Free Press/Free People*. New York: Columbia Univer-
    sity Press, 1971.
Homet, Roland S., Jr. *Politics, Cultures and Communication: European vs.
    American Approaches to Communications Policymaking*. New York:
    Praeger Special Studies, 1979.
Horvat, Branko; Markovic, Mihailo; and Supek, Rudi, eds. *Self-Govern-
    ing Socialism*. 2 vols. White Plains, N.Y.: International Arts and
    Sciences Press, 1975.
Howe, Irving. *Beyond the New Left*. New York: McCall, 1970.
————. *Steady Work: Essays in the Politics of Democratic Radicalism, 1953–
    66*. New York: Harcourt, Brace and World, 1966.
————, ed. *The Radical Imagination: An Anthology from Dissent Magazine*.
    New York: New American Library, 1967.
Howe, Irving, and Harrington, Michael. *The Seventies: Problems and
    Proposals*. New York: Harper and Row, 1972.
Hoyer, Svennik; Hadenius, Stig; and Weibull, Lennart. *The Politics and
    Economics of the Press: A Developmental Perspective*. Beverly Hills,
    Calif.: Sage Publications, 1975.
Hudson, Frederic. *Journalism in the United States: 1690–1872*. New York:
    Harper and Row, 1873.
Hulten, Olof. *Mass Media and State Support in Sweden*. Stockholm: The
    Swedish Institute, 1979.
Iben, Icko. *The Germanic Press of Europe*. Munich: Verlag C. J. Fahle,
    1965.
Immerwahr, John; Johnson, Jean; and Doble, John. *The Speaker and the
    Listener: A Public Perspective on Freedom of Expression*. New York:
    Public Agenda Foundation, 1980.
International Press Institute. *Government Pressures on the Press*. Zurich:
    International Press Institute, 1955.
Janda, Kenneth. *Political Parties: A Cross-national Survey*. New York: The
    Free Press, 1980.
Jessop, Bob. *The Capitalist State*. New York: New York University Press,
    1982.
Kaiser, Joseph H. *Press Planning: The State and Newspaper Publishing in
    Germany*. Zurich: International Press Institute, 1975.
Kautsky, Karl. *Das Erfurter Programm*. Stuttgart: J. H. W. Dietz, 1904.
Kesterton, W. H. *A History of Journalism in Canada*. Toronto: Mc-
    Clelland and Stewart, 1967.

Krieghbaum, Hillier. *Pressures on the Press*. New York: Thomas Crowell, 1972.

Kurian, George T., ed. *World Press Encyclopedia*. 2 vols. New York: Facts on File, 1982.

Landy, A. *Marxism and the Democratic Tradition*. New York: International Publishers, 1946.

Lee, Melvin. *History of American Journalism*. Boston: Houghton Mifflin, 1917.

Lenin, V. I. *Selected Works*. New York: International Publishers, 1919.

Lerner, Daniel, and Schramm, Wilbur. *Communication and Change in Developing Countries*. Honolulu: East-West Center Press, 1967.

Liebling, A. J. *The Press*. New York: Ballantine Books, 1975.

McCormick, Robert R. *The Freedom of the Press*. New York: Appleton-Century, 1936.

McPhail, Thomas L. *Electronic Colonialism: The Future of International Broadcasting and Communication*. Beverly Hills, Calif.: Sage Publications, 1981.

Mattelart, Armand. *Mass Media, Ideologies, and the Revolutionary Movement*. Atlantic Highlands, N.J.: Humanities Press, 1980.

Mattelart, Armand, and Siegelaub, Seth. *Communication and Class Struggle*. New York: International General, 1979.

Merrill, John C. *The Imperative of Freedom*. New York: Hastings House, 1974.

Merrill, John C., and Fischer, Harold A. *The World's Great Dailies*. New York: Hastings House, 1980.

Merrill, John C., and Lowenstein, Ralph. *Media, Messages and Men*. New York: David McKay, 1971.

———. *Media, Messages and Men*. 2nd ed. New York: Longman, 1979.

Mosco, Vincent, and Herman, Andrew. "Radical Social Theory and the Communications Revolution." In *Communication and Social Structure*, ed. Emile G. McAnany, Jorge Schnitman, and Noreen Janus, 58–84. New York: Praeger, 1981.

Mott, Frank L. *American Journalism, A History: 1690–1960*. 3rd ed. New York: Macmillan, 1962.

Mowlana, Hamid. "A Paradigm for Comparative Mass Media Analysis." In *International and Intercultural Communication*, ed. H. D. Fischer and J. C. Merrill, 474–484. New York: Hastings House, 1978.

Muller, Hans D. *Press Power. A Study of Axel Springer*. London: MacDonald, 1969.

Niebuhr, Reinhold, and Sigmund, Paul E. *The Democratic Experience: Past and Prospects*. New York: Praeger, 1969.

Nisbet, Robert. *The Social Philosophers*. New York: Thomas Crowell, 1973.

Olson, Kenneth. *The History Makers: The Press of Europe from Its Beginning through 1965*. Baton Rouge: Louisiana State University Press, 1966.

Owen, Bruce. *Economics and Freedom of Expression*. Cambridge, Mass.: Ballinger Publishing Co., 1975.

Palmer, R. R. *The Age of Democratic Revolution*. Princeton: Princeton University Press, 1959.

Parenti, Michael. *Democracy for the Few*. New York: St. Martin's Press, 1974.

Pateman, Carole. *Participation and Democratic Theory*. Cambridge: Cambridge University Press, 1970.

Payne, George H. *A History of Journalism in the United States*. New York: Appleton-Century, 1920.

Peterson, Theodore B.; Jenson, Jay W.; and Rivers, William L. *The Mass Media and Modern Society*. New York: Holt, Rinehart and Winston, 1965.

Rivers, William L. and Schramm, Wilbur. *Responsibility in Mass Communication*. Rev. ed. New York: Harper and Row, 1969.

Rousseau, Jean-Jacques. *On the Social Contract*. Trans. Judith Masters, ed. Roger Masters. New York: St. Martin's Press, 1978.

Ryan, Alan, ed. *The Idea of Freedom: Essays in Honour of Isaiah Berlin*. Oxford: Oxford University Press, 1979.

Salmon, Lucy Maynard. *The Newspaper and Authority*. New York: Oxford University Press, 1923.

———. *The Newspaper and the Historian*. New York: Oxford University Press, 1923.

Sanford, John. *The Mass Media in German-Speaking Countries*. London: Oswald Wolff, 1976.

Sartori, Giovanni. *Democratic Theory*. New York: Praeger, 1965.

Schiller, Dan. *Objectivity and the News: The Public and the Rise of Commercial Journalism*. Philadelphia: University of Pennsylvania Press, 1981.

Schiller, Herbert I. *Communication and Cultural Domination*. White Plains, N.Y.: M. E. Sharpe, 1976.

———. *Mass Communication and American Empire*. New York: Augustus Kelly, 1969.

———. *Who Knows: Information in the Age of the Fortune 500*. Norwood, N.J.: Ablex Publishing Co., 1981.

Schumpeter, Joseph A. *Capitalism, Socialism, and Democracy*. 5th ed. London: Allen and Unwin, 1956.

Schwoebel, Jean. *Newsroom Democracy: The Case for Independence of the*

Press. Iowa City: University of Iowa School of Journalism and Mass Communication, 1976.

Shub, David, and Shaplen, Joseph, eds. *Social Democracy versus Communism.* New York: Rand School Press, 1946.

Siebert, Frederick S. *Freedom of the Press in England, 1476–1776.* Urbana, Ill.: University of Illinois Press, 1952.

Siebert, Frederick S.; Peterson, Theodore; and Schramm, Wilbur. *Four Theories of the Press.* Urbana, Ill.: University of Illinois Press, 1956.

Singleton, Derrick. *Freedom of Communication.* London: Ampersand, 1963.

Smith, Anthony. *The Geopolitics of Information: Problems of Policy in Modern Media.* London: Macmillan, 1978.

————. *Goodbye Gutenberg.* New York: Oxford University Press, 1980.

————. *The Newspaper: An International History.* London: Thames and Hudson, 1979.

————. *Newspapers and Democracy.* Cambridge, Mass.: The MIT Press, 1980.

Smith, Culver H. *The Press, Politics and Patronage: The American Government's Use of Newspapers, 1789–1875.* Athens, Ga.: University of Georgia Press, 1977.

Stangerup, H., and Poulsen, E. *Newspapers in Denmark.* Copenhagen: Det Danske Selskab, 1953.

Stevens, David H. *Party Politics and English Journalism, 1702–1742.* New York: Russell and Russell, 1916. Reissued 1967.

Stromberg, Andrew. *A History of Sweden.* New York: Macmillan Co., 1931. Reprint. New York: Kraus Reprint Co., 1969.

Szecsko, Tamas. "The Development of a Socialist Communication Theory." In *Mass Media Policies in Changing Cultures,* ed. George Gerbner, 223–234. New York: John Wiley and Sons, 1977.

Tebbel, John. *The Compact History of the American Newspaper.* New York: Hawthorn Books, 1963.

Thorsen, Svend. *Newspapers in Denmark.* Copenhagen: Det Danske Selskab, 1953.

Twentieth Century Fund Taskforce on the International Flow of News. *A Free and Balanced Flow.* Lexington, Mass.: Lexington Books, 1978.

Vanek, Jaroslav. *The Participatory Economy: An Evolutionary Hypothesis and a Strategy for Development.* Ithaca, N.Y.: Cornell University Press, 1971.

————. *Self Management: Economic Liberation of Man.* Baltimore: Penguin Books, 1975.

Williams, Francis. *The Right to Know: The Rise of the World Press.* London: Longmans, Green and Co., 1969.

Williams, Herbert Lee. *Newspaper Organization and Management.* 5th ed. Ames, Iowa: Iowa State University Press, 1978.

ARTICLES

Andren, Nils. "Sweden: State Support for Political Parties." *Scandinavian Political Studies* 3 (1968): 221–229.

Bagdikian, Ben. "Newspaper Mergers—The Final Phase." *Columbia Journalism Review* 15 (March/April 1977): 17–22.

———. "Why Dailies Die." *New Republic* 146 (April 16, 1962): 17–23.

Barber, Benjamin. "The Second American Revolution: The Wired Republic May Prove Hazardous to Democracy." *Channels of Communications* 1 (Feb./March 1982): 21+.

Barnett, Stephen R. "Media Monopoly and the Law." *Journal of Communication* 30 (Spring 1980): 72–80.

Barron, Jerome. "Access to the Press: A New First Amendment Right." *Harvard Law Review* 80 (June 1967): 1641.

Beckett, Francis. "IFJ Looks at Concentration of Western Press Ownership." *Media Law Reporter* 5 (Autumn 1981): 41.

Bishop, Robert L. "Can Governments Pay the Piper without Calling the Tune?" *IPI Report* 19 (August 1970): 1–4.

Bishop, Robert L.; Sharma, Katherine; and Brazee, Richard J. "Determinants of Newspaper Circulation: A Pooled Cross-sectional Time Series Study in the United States, 1850–1970." *Communication Research* 7 (January 1980): 3–22.

Bissland, J. H. "Denmark, Norway Papers Need Financial Assistance." *Editor and Publisher* 108 (Oct. 25, 1975): 41–42.

Bourroughs, Elise. "Degree of Freedom Varies for 'Free Press.' " *Presstime* 4 (April 1982): 9.

Brown, Dennis, and Merrill, John C. "Regulatory Pluralism in the Press." *Freedom of Information Center Report* 5 (Oct. 1965): 1–4.

Brown, Robert U. "Shop Talk at Thirty: Press Subsidies." *Editor and Publisher* 107 (May 11, 1974): 80.

Bryan, Carter R. "Enlightenment of the People without Hindrance: The Swedish Press Law of 1766." *Journalism Quarterly* 37 (Summer 1960): 431–434.

———. "Local Pride and Social Responsibility Keep Sweden's Grassroots Press Alive." *Grassroots Editor* (April 1961): 15.

"Can Newspapers Beat Rising Costs?" *IPI Report* 13 (Aug./Sept. 1964): 17–21.

Coase, R. H. "The Economics of the First Amendment: The Market for Goods and the Market for Ideas." *American Economic Review* 64 (May 1974): 384–391.

"Covert Charge." *The Nation* 234 (June 19, 1982): 738.
"Effects of Growing Dependence on Government Aid." *IPI Report* 25 (April 1976): 18–19.
Engwall, Lars. "Newspaper Concentration: A Case for Theories of Oligopoly." *Scandinavian Economic History Review* 29 (Fall 1981): 145–154.
————. "The Structure of the Swedish Daily Press." *Swedish Journal of Economics* 77 (1975): 318–328.
Ferguson, Thomas, and Rogers, Joel. "Oligopoly in the Idea Market." *The Nation* 233 (Oct. 3, 1981): 303–308.
Fjaestad, Bjorn, and Holmlov, P. G. "Swedish Newsmen's Views on the Role of the Press." *Studier i Ekonomisk Psykologi* 7 (1975): 1–60.
Fleisher, Frederic. "The Swedish Press Subsidy Plan and the Collapse of Stockholms-Tidningen." *Gazette* 12 (1966): 179–186.
Furhoff, Lars. "Some Reflections on Newspaper Concentration." *Scandinavian Economic History Review* 21 (1973): 1–27.
"Government Loan Proposed to Help Press in Sweden." *Editor and Publisher* (Dec. 28, 1968): 17.
Gustafsson, Karl Erik. "The Circulation Spiral and the Principle of Household Coverage." *Scandinavian Economic History Review* 26 (1978): 1–14.
Hadenius, Stig. "Mass Media and the State in Sweden." *Gazette* 23 (1977): 105–115.
Hadenius, Stig; Sveveborg, Jean-Olof; and Weibull, Lennart. "The Social Democratic Press and Newspaper Policy in Sweden, 1899–1909." *Scandinavian Political Studies* 3 (1968): 49–69.
Hall, John R. "The Time of History and the History of the Times." *History and Theory* 19 (1980): 113–131.
Hemanus, Pertti. "Development Trends in the Scandinavian Press." *Gazette* 17 (1971): 1–15.
Henderson, Hazel. "Access to the Media: A Problem in Democracy." *Columbia Jounalism Review* 8 (Spring 1969): 5–8.
Hollstein, Milton. "Are Newspaper Subsidies Unthinkable?" *Columbia Journalism Review* 17 (May/June 1978): 15–18.
————. "Government and the Press: The Question of Subsidies." *Journal of Communication* 28 (Autumn 1978): 46–53.
"How Shah Used Cash to Bring Iran's Press to Heel." *IPI Report* 28 (January 1979): 16.
Hoyer, Svennik. "The Political Economy of the Norwegian Press." *Scandinavian Political Studies* 3 (1968): 85–143.
Jacklin, Phil. "A New Fairness Doctrine: Access to the Media." *The Center Magazine* 8 (May/June 1975): 46–50.

James, Beverly. "Economic Democracy and Restructuring the Press."
    Journal of Communication Inquiry 6 (Winter 1981): 119–129.

Keep, Paul M. "Newspaper Preservation Act Update." *Freedom of In-
    formation Center Report* 456 (May 1982): 1–7.

Koether, George. "Free Market and Free Press." *Freedom of Information
    Center Report* 31 (July 1960): 1–5.

Kristjansson, Jonas. "State Pays the Piper but Parties Call the Tune."
    IPI Report 25 (Oct. 1976): 9.

Labrado, Francisco Garcia. "Condicionamientos del Problema de la
    Ayuda Economica Estatal a la Prensa en Estados Unidos." *Re-
    vista Espanola de la Opinion Publica* 35 (Enero-Marzo 1974): 123–
    152.

———. "Presupuestos Ideologicos y Modalidades de la Ayuda Estatal
    a la Prensa." *Revista Espanola de la Opinion Publica* 30 (Octubre-
    Diciembre 1972): 3–34.

"La Prensa Loses Advertising." *IPI Report* 30 (July 1981): 5.

Lasch, Christopher. "Mass Culture Revisited." *democracy* 1 (Oct. 1981).

Lent, John. "Caribbean Press Hemmed In with Controls." *IPI Report*
    25 (Sept. 1976): 1–2+.

Lewels, Joel, Jr. "The Newspaper Preservation Act." *Freedom of Infor-
    mation Center Report* 254 (Jan. 1971): 1–5.

Lidbom, Carl. "Government Provides Subsidy for the Press in Swe-
    den." *Grassroots Editor* 15 (Jan.-Feb. 1974): 28–29.

Lieberman, J. Ben. "Restating the Concept of Freedom of the Press."
    Journalism Quarterly 30 (Spring 1953): 131–138.

McCarthy, John. "Direct Subsidization: A Tonic for the Weak or an
    Anesthetic for All?" *IPI Report* 25 (Oct. 1976): 9–10.

McDonald, Donald. "The Media's Conflicts of Interest." *The Center
    Magazine* 9 (Nov./Dec. 1976): 15–35.

Merrill, John C. "The Press and Social Responsibility." *Freedom of In-
    formation Center Opinion Paper* 1 (March 1965): 1–3.

Nenning, Gunther. "Negative and Positive Press Freedom." *IPI Report*
    15 (Sept. 1966):8.

Nixon, Raymond. "Freedom in the World's Press: A Fresh Appraisal
    with Data." *Journalism Quarterly* 42 (Winter 1965): 3–14.

Nixon, Raymond, and Han, Tae-goul. "Concentration of Press Own-
    ership: A Comparison of Thirty-two Countries." *Journalism
    Quarterly* 48 (Spring 1971): 5–16.

Nordenstreng, Kaarle. "Recent Developments in European Commu-
    nications Theory." *Journal of Communication Inquiry* 2 (Winter
    1977): 41–50.

Nortamo, Simopekka. "Helsingin Sanomat Editor Warns That Selec-
    tive Forms of Government Subsidies to Newspapers Constitute

Real Threat to Freedom of the Press." *IPI Report* 26 (Jan. 1977): 9+.

"Norway." *IPI Report* 25 (April 1976): 4–5.

Novitz, Charles. "Is It Time for a News Subsidy?" *The Quill* 70 (Oct. 1982): 29.

Nycanter, Svante. "The Case for Press Subsidies." *IPI Report* 14 (June 1965): 3.

Ostgaard, Einer. "Effects of Growing Dependence on Government Aid: Analysis of Official Reports Published in Norway and Sweden." *IPI Report* 25 (April 1976): 18–19.

———. "Swedish Press Subsidies Go Up Forty Per Cent." *IPI Report* 25 (Aug. 1976): 11.

Pers, Anders Y. "The Case against (Press Subsidies)." *IPI Report* 25 (Aug. 1976): 3.

Picard, Robert G. "A Change of Course for Swedish Subsidies." *IPI Report* 29 (Nov. 1980): 11–13.

———. "Positive Liberty and the Press." *Scholar and Educator* (Fall 1982): 31–35.

———. "State Aid and Newspaper Marketing in Two Swedish Cities, 1965–1978." *Gazette* 28 (1981): 17–33.

———. "State Intervention in U.S. Press Economics." *Gazette* 30 (1983): 3–11.

———. "Sweden Boosts Weeklies." *Grassroots Editor* 21 (Spring 1980): 12–13.

Pietila, Antero. "Swedish Editors' Views on Government Support of the Press." *Journalism Quarterly* 48 (Winter 1979): 724–729.

Prinsky, Robert. "Europe's Hard Up Newspapers." *Wall Street Journal* (Sept. 15, 1975): 10.

Salmelin, Pertti. "The Transition of the Finnish Workers' Papers to the Social Democratic Press." *Scandinavian Political Studies* 3 (1968): 70–84.

Schwoebel, Jean. "The Miracle 'Le Monde' Wrought." *Columbia Journalism Review* 9 (Summer 1970): 8–9.

Slade, Clyde M. "Daily Newspapers and Social Accountability." *Journal of Communication Inquiry* 5 (Winter 1980): 43–53.

"Slow Squeeze on the Greek Press." *IPI Report* 18 (March 1970): 1.

Smith, Anthony. "Subsidies and the Press in Europe." *Political and Economic Planning* vol. 43, no. 569 (1977): 1–113.

———. "Who's Afraid of Handouts?" *IPI Report* 26 (May/June 1977): 21–22.

Smythe, Dallas W. "On the Political Economy of Communications." *Journalism Quarterly* 37 (Autumn 1969): 563–572.

"The Sporting Life." *The Progressive* (Jan. 1983): 11.

"The State: Old Enemy or New Savior." *IPI Report* 16 (Feb. 1967): 8–10.

Steinby, Torsten. "Escape Routes." *IPI Report* 16 (Nov. 1967): 9–10.

———. "Press Subsidies." *IPI Report* 17 (April 1965): 3.

"The Struggle Goes On over State Taxes." *Presstime* 3 (Dec. 1981): 16.

"Subsidies and Press Freedom." *IPI Report* 15 (March 1967): 6.

"Subsidy Principle Accepted but. . . . " *IPI Report* 24 (Nov. 1975): 8–10.

Tate, Cassandra. "Gannett in Salem: Protecting the Franchise. . . . " *Columbia Journalism Review* 20 (July/August 1981): 51–56.

Thomsen, Niels. "The Danish Political Press." *Scandinavian Political Studies* 3 (1968): 144–164.

Thomsen, Per. "Norway." *IPI Report* 26 (April 1977): 4–5.

———. "Norway: Looking Out After Number Two." *IPI Report* 15 (Nov. 1967): 10–11.

" 'Vulnerable'—That's the Press in Europe." *IPI Report* 27 (June 1978): 2.

Wahlgren, Olof. "Press Subsidies: Swedish Case." *IPI Report* 23 (Feb. 1974): 1–2.

Wilhoit, Cleveland, and Drew, Dan. "A Profile of the Editorial Writer." *Masthead* (Fall 1971): 2–14.

Zeicher, Barrie. "Reflections on the Kent Commission." *Content* (Jan./Feb. 1982): 7.

GOVERNMENT REPORTS AND DOCUMENTS

Canada. *Report of the Royal Commission on Newspapers.* Hull, Quebec: Canadian Government Printing Centre, 1981.

Commission of the European Communities. *Evolution of Concentration and Competition in the Danish Newspaper and Magazine Sector.* Evolution of Concentration and Competition Series, no. 10. Brussels: Commission of the European Communities, May 1978.

———. *Evolution de la Concentration et de la Concurrence de la Presse en Belgique.* Evolution of Concentration and Competition Series, no. 11. Brussels: Commission of the European Communities, May 1978.

———. *Evolution de la Concentration dans l'industrie de la Presse en France.* Evolution of Concentration and Competition Series, no. 7. Brussels: Commission of the European Communities, January 1978.

———. *Studio Sull'evoluzione della Concentrazione nei Settori dell'edizione e della Stampa in Italia, 1968–1975.* Evolution of Concentration and

Competition Series, no. 3. Brussels: Commission of the European Communities, 1978.

————. *A Study of the Evolution of Concentration in the Dutch Press, Magazine and Schoolbooks Publishing Industries.* Evolution of Concentration and Competition Series, no. 16. Brussels: Commission of the European Communities, June 1978.

————. *A Study of the Evolution of Concentration in the Irish Publishing Industry.* Evolution of Concentration and Competition Series, no. 14. Brussels: Commission of the European Communities, May 1978.

————. *A Study of the Evolution of Concentration in the Press and General Publishing Industry of the United Kingdom.* Evolution of Concentration and Competition Series, no. 1. Brussels: Commission of the European Communities, October 1977.

————. *Untersuchung zur Konzentrationsentwicklung im Presse- und Verlagswesen der Bundesrepublik Deutschland.* Evolution of Concentration and Competition Series, no. A19. Brussels: Commission of the European Communities, September 1978.

Council of Europe. Resolution 43 (1974) on Press Concentration.

————. Resolution 834 (1978) on Threats to Freedom of the Press.

————. Committee of Experts on Press Concentration. "Working Paper on the Scope of Press Concentration and Measures of Economic Assistance." Unpublished report. Strasbourg, 1971.

Denmark. Mediekommissionens. *Betaenkning om de Trykte Mediers Okonomi og Beskaeftigelse.* Bataenkning nr. 972, 1983. Aarhus: Aarhus Stiftsbogtrykkerie, 1983.

Finland. *Part I and II of the Report of the Government Committee on Communication Policy. Investigations and Recommendations concerning the Press and News Agencies.* Abridged. Committee Reports 1973:91 I and 1973:91 II, abridged. Helsinki: Government Printing Centre, 1983.

France. "Rapport du Groupe de Travail sur les Aides Publiques aux Enterprises de Presse." Unpublished report. Paris, 1972.

Germany, Federal Republic of. *Final Report of the Press Commission.* BT Drucks V/3122, June 14, 1968.

Norway. *Massemedier og Mediepolitik.* NOU 1983:3.

————. *Rapporten om Massemedier.* NOU 1982:30. Oslo: Universitetsforlaget, 1982.

Sweden. Budget Departementet. *Oversyn av Presstodet* 10 (1978).

————. Finansdepartementet. *Svensk Press: Pressens Funktioner i Samhallet* SOU 1975:8.

————. Finansdepartementet. *Presstodet och Tidningskonkurrensen* SOU 1974:102.

————. Finansdepartementet. *Svensk Press: Statlig Press Politik* SOU 1975:79.

————. Finansdepartementet. *Svensk Press: Tidningar i Samverkan* SOU 1975:11.

————. Justitiedepartementet. *Beskrivning och analys* SOU 1972:7.

————. Justitiedepartementet. *Dagspressens Situation* SOU 1968:48.

————. Justitiedepartementet. *Dagstidningarnas Ekonomiska Villkor* SOU 1965:22.

————. Justitiedepartementet. *Massmediegrundlag* SOU 1975:49.

————. Presstodsnamnden. *Dagspressrapport* 1977:1.

UNESCO. International Commission for the Study of Communication Problems. *Many Voices, One World.* New York: Unipub, 1980.

United Kingdom. Royal Commission on the Press. *Interim Report on the National Newspaper Industry.* London: Her Majesty's Stationery Office, March 1976.

————. Royal Commission on the Press. "Press Subsidies in Foreign Countries." Unpublished report, May 1976.

————. Royal Commission on the Press. *Report of the Royal Commission on the Press.* Cmnd 6810. London: Her Majesty's Stationery Office, 1974.

United States of America. Federal Trade Commission, Bureau of Competition. *Proceedings of the Symposium on Media Concentration: December 14 and 15, 1978.* 2 vols. Washington, D.C.: Government Printing Office, 1980.

————. National Commission on the Causes and Prevention of Violence. *Mass Media and Violence.* Washington, D.C.: Government Printing Office, 1969.

UNPUBLISHED MATERIALS

Bishop, Robert. "Modernization and the European Press." Paper presented at the annual meeting of the Association for Education in Journalism, Lawrence, Kan., 1968.

Bissland, James H. "Reforming the Press: The Democratic Alternative to News Media Bureaucracy." Ph.D. diss., University of Iowa, 1976.

Braun, Lars. "Press Subsidies in the Nordic Countries." Paper presented to the 11th Congress of the International Association for Mass Communication Research, Warsaw, Poland, 1978.

Choo, Kwang Yung. "Dimensions of Press Control: A Factor Analytic Study of National Characteristics and Press Systems of the World." Ph.D. diss., University of Texas, 1976.

Gustafsson, Karl Erik. "Press Research and Press Subsidies in Sweden." Mimeo report of the Department of Business Administration, University of Gothenburg, Sweden, 1979.
Halloran, James D. "Monitoring Media Policy and Performance Internationally." Paper presented at the World Media Conference,
New York, Oct. 1–4, 1981.
Hardt, Hanno, and James, Beverly. "Newspapers and Western Democracies: Towards a Participatory Model of the Press." Paper
presented at the Sixth National Conference of the Society of Ed-
ucators and Scholars, Champaign-Urbana, Ill., Oct. 1–2, 1981.
Lowenstein, Ralph L. "Measuring World Press Freedom as a Political
Indicator." Ph.D. diss., University of Missouri-Columbia, 1967.
McLuskie, Ed. "Systematic Constraints on Prospects for a Democratic
Society: Basic Considerations from the Communication Theory
of Society." Paper presented at the Sixth National Conference
of the Society of Educators and Scholars, Champaign-Urbana,
Ill., Oct. 1–2, 1981.
Parsons, Patrick R. "Economics of the Newspaper Industry: A Marx-
ian Analysis." M.A. thesis, California State University, North-
ridge, 1978.
Picard, Robert G. "Government Subsidies and Press Freedom in Swe-
den." Paper presented at the Far West Regional Meeting of
Women in Communications, Inc., Irvine, Calif., 1980.
———. "Influences on State Intervention in Press Economics: A
Regression Analysis." Paper presented at the Western Com-
munications Educators Conference, California State University,
Fullerton, Nov. 5, 1983.
———. "Promoting Democracy: Development of the Theory of Posi-
tive Press Freedom." Paper presented at the Sixth National
Conference of the Society of Educators and Scholars, Cham-
paign-Urbana, Ill., Oct. 1–2, 1981.
———. "State Aid and the Press: A Case Study of Newspapers in Two
Swedish Cities, 1965–1978." M.A. thesis, California State Uni-
versity, Fullerton, 1979.
———. "State Intervention in Press Economics in Advanced Western
Democratic Nations." Ph.D. diss., University of Missouri-Co-
lumbia, 1983.
Pietila, Antero. "Government Subsidies and Press Freedom: The Case
of Sweden." M.A. thesis, Southern Illinois University, 1969.
Ramos, Murilo C. O. "News, Class, and Ideology: A Study of Labor
Coverage in Two Elite Brazilian Newspapers." Ph.D. diss.,
University of Missouri-Columbia, 1982.

Yodelis, Mary Ann. "Boston's Second Major Paper War: Economics,
     Politics, and the Theory and Practice of Political Expression in
     the Press, 1763–1775." Ph.D. diss., University of Wisconsin, 1971.
————. "Economics and the Boston, Massachusetts, Newspapers—
     1763–1775." M.A. thesis, University of Wisconsin, 1969.
————. "Religion Paid the Piper, but Politicians Called the Tune." Pa-
     per presented at the University of Maryland Bicentennial Sym-
     posium, April 23, 1976.

Index

Index

171

Italy, 103, 108, 116, 117, 120, 121,
127

Kautsky, Karl, 28
Kent Commission, 146

Labor costs, 15, 105
Labour Party, 28
Liberals, 76
Libertarians, 15, 26; pseudo-lib-
ertarians, 45
Libertarianism, Anglo-American,
17-18
Liberties, 6, 11, 13
Liberty: contradictions with
equality, 6-7; negative, 35, 39,
40, 48; positive, 39, 40, 48, 50
Liebling, A. J., 47
Loans to media, 18, 83, 106, 109,
144, 149
Locke, John, 11, 39
Lowenstein, Ralph, 64, 109

Mandel, Ernest, 43, 81, 85-86
Marketplace of goods and ser-
vices, 14, 89, 135
Marketplace of ideas, 12-15, 25,
43, 89, 134, 145; constraints
on, 14-15, 18-19, 133-35, 146
Marx, Karl: and democracy, 32-
33; on press freedom, 38
Marxists, 141; neo-Marxists, 35
Merrill, John C., 15, 45-46, 63-64,
77
Mill, James, 45
Mill, John Stuart, 45
Milton, John, 12-13, 16
Minority, 49, 78, 84; interests,
15, 140; rights, 7-8, 11; tyranny
of, 11
Monarchies, 6, 13
Monopoly, newspaper, 17, 60
Mortality, newspaper, 17, 43, 44,

57, 66, 76, 84, 105, 125, 127,
134

National Commission on the
Causes and Prevention of Vio-
lence, 80
National Endowment for the Hu-
manities, 102
Nationalist movements, 65
Nation-state, 41
Nenning, Gunther, 44-45
Netherlands, the, 58, 105, 116,
117, 120, 121, 127
New Federalism, 87
News agency aid, 107
Newspaper Preservation Act,
112, 144
Newspapers, role of, 3, 4, 37-38
Newsroom autonomy and de-
mocracy, 78-79
Nonaligned Movement, 61
Nordenstreng, Kaarle, 47, 135,
137
Norway, 105, 106-7, 116, 117,
120, 121, 122, 127

Objective theory, 132-33
On the Social Contract (Rousseau),
39
Ownership of newspapers: concentration of, 19, 35, 43, 44,
58-59, 66, 76, 84, 88, 131, 134-
35, 146; regulation of, 26, 107,
120, 148; types under democratic socialism, 67, 81-82, 85-
86, 92, 148

Parsons, Patrick, 59, 135
Participation, 10, 26, 27, 33-34,
73, 136, 146
Plurality: communicator, 59; media, 18, 74, 76-77, 113, 148;
message, 18, 59

About the Author

ROBERT G. PICARD, Assistant Professor in the Manship School of Journalism at Louisiana State University, has both professional and academic experience in the field of journalism. He has written articles for such scholarly journals as *Journalism Quarterly, Gazette, Newspaper Research Journal, Journal of Communication Inquiry,* and *Mass Comm Review.*